Will the Scientific and Technology Workforce Meet the Requirements of the Federal Government?

WILLIAM P. BUTZ, TERRENCE K. KELLY, DAVID M. ADAMSON,
GABRIELLE A. BLOOM, DONNA FOSSUM, MIHAL E. GROSS

Prepared for the Office of Science and Technology Policy

SCIENCE AND TECHNOLOGY

The research described in this report was conducted by the Science and Technology Policy Institute (operated by RAND from 1992 to November 2003) for the Office of Science and Technology Policy, under contract ENG-9812731.

Library of Congress Cataloging-in-Publication Data

Will the scientific & technical workforce meet the requirements of the federal government? / William P. Butz ... [et al.].
    p. cm.
    "MG-118."
    Includes bibliographical references.
    ISBN 0-8330-3529-0
    1. Scientists—United States. 2. Engineers—United States. 3. Technologists—United States. 4. United States—Officials and employees. I. Title: Will the scientific and technical workforce meet the requirements of the federal government?. II. Butz, William P.

Q149.U5W55 2004
331.7'615'0973—dc22

2003024741

The RAND Corporation is a nonprofit research organization providing objective analysis and effective solutions that address the challenges facing the public and private sectors around the world. RAND's publications do not necessarily reflect the opinions of its research clients and sponsors.

RAND® is a registered trademark.

Published 2004 by the RAND Corporation
1700 Main Street, P.O. Box 2138, Santa Monica, CA 90407-2138
1200 South Hayes Street, Arlington, VA 22202-5050
201 North Craig Street, Suite 202, Pittsburgh, PA 15213-1516
RAND URL: http://www.rand.org/
To order RAND documents or to obtain additional information, contact
Distribution Services: Telephone: (310) 451-7002;
Fax: (310) 451-6915; Email: order@rand.org

Preface

About This Report

The size and adequacy of the federal government's workforce for carrying out scientific, technical, engineering, and mathematics (STEM) activities are recurring concerns in many policy circles. This report presents the results of a study that examined the current federal STEM workforce. The authors assess whether personnel shortages or other deficiencies in the federal STEM workforce may be imminent, examine legislation and programs implemented in the past to identify measures that might be instituted now, and explore the data that the federal government needs to collect to monitor this issue adequately.

The research for this study was sponsored by the Office of Science and Technology Policy. This report should be of interest to the science and technology policy community, science and math educators, and students assessing alternative training and career paths.

About the Science and Technology Policy Institute

Originally created by Congress in 1991 as the Critical Technologies Institute and renamed in 1998, the Science and Technology Policy Institute (S&TPI) is a federally funded research and development center sponsored by the National Science Foundation. The S&TPI was managed by RAND from 1992 through November 30, 2003.

The Institute's mission is to help improve public policy by conducting objective, independent research and analysis on policy issues that involve science and technology. To this end, the Institute

- supports the Office of Science and Technology Policy and other Executive Branch agencies, offices, and councils
- helps science and technology decisionmakers understand the likely consequences of their decisions and choose among alternative policies
- helps improve understanding in both the public and private sectors of the ways in which science and technology can better serve national objectives.

In carrying out its mission, the Institute consults broadly with representatives from private industry, institutions of higher education, and other nonprofit institutions.

Inquiries regarding the work described in this report may be directed to:

Stephen Rattien
Director
RAND Science and Technology
1200 South Hayes Street
Arlington, VA 22202-5050
703-413-1100, ext. 5219
Web: www.rand.org/scitech

The RAND Corporation Quality Assurance Process

Peer review is an integral part of all RAND research projects. Prior to publication, this document, as with all documents in the RAND monograph series, was subject to a quality assurance process to ensure that the research meets several standards, including the following: The problem is well formulated; the research approach is well designed and well executed; the data and assumptions are sound; the findings are useful and advance knowledge; the implications and recommendations follow logically from the findings and are explained thoroughly; the documentation is accurate, understandable, cogent, and temperate in tone; the research demonstrates understanding of related previous studies; and the research is relevant, objective, independent, and balanced. Peer review is conducted by research professionals who were not members of the project team.

RAND routinely reviews and refines its quality assurance process and also conducts periodic external and internal reviews of the quality of its body of work. For additional details regarding the RAND quality assurance process, visit http://www.rand.org/standards/.

Contents

Figures

Summary

The federal government relies on technically trained personnel to carry out a variety of critical functions in several mission areas, including national defense, homeland security, health, space, transportation, and agriculture. Recently, the size and adequacy of the federal workforce for carrying out scientific, technical, engineering, and mathematics (STEM) activities have become areas of concern in many policy circles. Knowledgeable sources both inside and outside of government have voiced fears that this workforce is aging and may soon face a dwindling labor pool, a problem that could be compounded by skill shortages in key areas and a growing proportion of non-U.S. citizens obtaining STEM degrees in the United States.

This report assesses the condition of the federal STEM workforce,[1] based on the best data available, and also discusses the data that would be required for a more comprehensive analysis. The report examines three issues:

---

[1] This research does not address the specific composition or diversity of the federal STEM workforce with the one exception of a brief look at the need for citizen versus non-citizen workers. It was developed based on available data and interviews with representatives from nine federal departments, agencies, or offices: the Departments of Homeland Security, Energy, Transportation, Health and Human Services (to include representatives from the Centers for Disease Control and Prevention and the Agency for Toxic Substances and Disease Registry), and Agriculture, the National Aeronautics and Space Administration, the National Science Foundation, the Office of Personnel Management, and the Office of Management and Budget.

- Broader trends in the U.S. STEM workforce that might affect the federal STEM workforce
- Trends and workforce-shaping activities in the federal STEM workforce
- Legislative and programmatic mechanisms for influencing the federal STEM workforce.

To address these issues, a RAND Corporation team reviewed the relevant literature and data on STEM education, labor force, and labor markets. The team also collected data and interviewed STEM managers at selected federal agencies, including the National Aeronautics and Space Administration (NASA), the National Institutes of Health (NIH), and the Departments of Agriculture, Energy, Defense, Homeland Security, and Transportation, the Office of Management and Budget, and the Office of Personnel Management.

Background: Are There Looming Shortages in the U.S. STEM Workforce?

If there are looming personnel shortages in or skill mismatches for the federal STEM workforce, these problems might be reflected in broader U.S. STEM workforce data and trends.[2] Therefore, the first phase of our analysis is an examination of the broader U.S. STEM workforce. We focused on whether economic indicators point to shortages of U.S. STEM workers in the recent past, at present, or in the near future.

Data Sources and Limitations

At the time of this research, which was conducted in 2003, much of the available data on STEM personnel in the U.S. workforce were

---

[2] Different concepts of "shortage"—what it is and how to measure it—underlie much past discussion of the topic of this report, even though authors and commentators have often neglected to define their particular concepts. This report attempts to be clear about particular concepts, following the alternative concepts defined and analyzed in Butz et al. (2003).

available only up to the year 2000. Hence, the effects of both the collapse of the Internet "bubble" and the recession of 2002 are not reflected here. These events presumably slowed or reduced the demand for STEM personnel compared with expectations derived from this analysis.

Findings

Despite recurring concerns about potential shortages of STEM personnel in the U.S. workforce, particularly in engineering and information technology, we did not find evidence that such shortages have existed at least since 1990, nor that they are on the horizon.

If there were shortages of STEM workers, we would expect these shortages to be reflected in certain economic indicators, most notably low levels of unemployment and rising wages for STEM workers. However, in examining earning patterns and employment patterns for STEM workers, we found no patterns that were consistent with a shortage of STEM workers. The statistics do not portray the kinds of vigorous earnings and employment prospects that would be expected to draw increasing numbers of workers into STEM fields.

Likewise, "underemployment patterns"—indications of STEM workers involuntarily working out of their fields—suggest that underemployment of STEM workers is relatively high compared with non-STEM workers. Engineering is an exception—its underemployment rate has been lower than that for non-STEM workers.

There are also concerns about the high proportion of non-citizens earning STEM degrees in the United States. These concerns typically center on potential shortages of U.S. citizens to fill security-related STEM jobs that require STEM degrees, or broader concerns that the United States could become too dependent on foreign STEM expertise. The non-citizen trend was up at least between 1970 and the mid-1990s. More recently in the half decade before 2000, the proportion leveled off. Overall, this growth was proportionally less than the growth of non-STEM Ph.D.s acquired by non-citizens. On the demand side, we do not foresee sufficient growth in the numbers of STEM workers who must have security clearances (and hence U.S. citizenship) to strain the numbers available.

Based on all of these indicators, we find neither an inadequate supply of STEM workers to supply the nation's current needs, nor indications of shortages in the foreseeable future. While it may be argued that any possibility of shortages must be met by accelerating the supply, the cost to young people of completing years of training only to emerge into labor markets with surplus STEM workers should also be considered. Over the past half century, the latter problem has occurred much more frequently than the former.[3]

The Federal STEM Workforce

With this context in mind, we collected data from federal agencies about their STEM workforces and solicited their perceptions of major problems and concerns.

Data Sources and Limitations

The federal Office of Personnel Management (OPM) keeps accurate data on the current federal STEM civil service workforce. However, federal agencies' forecasts of future needs are inadequate to inform current decisionmaking. An important trend in the federal STEM workforce is the increasing use of contract workers, rather than civil service employees, to perform federal STEM functions. Few agencies, NASA being the only exception that we found, keep adequate data on this workforce. Given these limitations, our analysis focused on the federal civil service STEM workforce.

Our interviews, along with data from the Office of Personnel Management, permit a more-timely portrait, however incomplete, of the federal STEM workforce than is available for the U.S. STEM workforce. In particular, initial effects of the collapse of the Internet bubble, the 2002 recession, and the terrorist attacks of September 11,

---

[3] Note that this statement does not claim that labor market conditions have not been generally good for STEM workers. Rather, it points out that the data indicate periodic surpluses and a softening of the market for important elements of the STEM workforce (see Chapter Two for details).

2001, are presumably incorporated in these data and in the expectations of federal STEM managers.

Findings

- There is evidence that the federal STEM workforce is aging. Department of Defense (DoD) data show that the percentage of its STEM workforce that is eligible to retire will more than double by 2012. Both NASA and NIH anticipate similar trends.
- However, older federal STEM workers tend to stay on for a longer period past retirement age than many other groups of workers. Hence, retirement eligibility is an unreliable harbinger of workforce shortages.
- Notwithstanding agency concerns about potential losses to retirement or a dwindling STEM workforce, the actual turnover rate for federal STEM workers is lower than that for the equivalent workforce in industry.
- STEM workers who do leave federal employment tend to be younger workers—in their 30s—who are headed for the "greener pastures" of industry rather than older workers entering retirement.
- The federal government tends to hire relatively older workers. For example, 70 percent of government hires in 2002 were over the age of 30. A substantial number of older STEM workers were hired by the federal government between 1997 and 2002.
- Workforce incentives are becoming more prominent as a way of attracting and retaining high-quality STEM workers. Some agencies have had success with these techniques and others anticipate using them more aggressively. NASA and the Centers for Disease Control and Prevention (CDC), for example, have obtained special authority from OPM to offer salaries above typical federal rates.
- A significant proportion of STEM workers employed on federal projects work in fact for private-sector contractors. This mechanism allows the government to reach flexibly into the private sector for more or fewer STEM workers as the requirements change. Accordingly, the workforce constraints become the size

and characteristics of the entire national STEM workforce, not just those who choose to be government employees.

- Although the proportion of STEM workers who require security clearances (and hence citizenship) may increase due to national defense and homeland security concerns, the actual numbers of such jobs are very small compared with the federal STEM workforce and with the number of STEM workers in the national workforce who are citizens. We do not foresee a shortage of STEM-trained citizens eligible for security clearance.

Legislative and Programmatic Mechanisms for Influencing the Federal STEM Workforce

We examined the policy mechanisms—including legislative initiatives, agency programs, and other means—by which the federal government influences both the national and the federal STEM workforce. We found virtually no measures that have specifically focused on the entire federal STEM workforce. Instead, most mechanisms have addressed aspects of the workforce (such as information technology workers) or specific agency needs.

We divided these mechanisms into two basic categories, "filling the pipeline"—mechanisms for attracting students into STEM fields and supporting their education and training, and "shaping the workforce"—mechanisms for recruiting, retaining, and developing the skills of STEM workers.

Filling the Pipeline

The goals of the pipeline-filling mechanisms are to attract students into STEM fields. These mechanisms are also used to address diversity issues by targeting underrepresented demographic groups, including ethnic minorities and women. These mechanisms include:

- General interest building: kindergarten through grade 12 (K–12) programs, summer institutes for teachers, university-school partnership programs, and other means for increasing interest and awareness in STEM careers.

- Counseling and guidance: programs that direct students into STEM careers. These include internships and apprenticeships.
- Resources for universities: the broad range of federal programs for supporting higher education, including grants, loans, assistantships, most of which are funded by the three federal agencies with a science education mission—the National Science Foundation (NSF), the NIH, and NASA.

Shaping the Workforce

The goals of the workforce-shaping mechanisms are to recruit, retain, and promote a quality STEM workforce. These mechanisms include:

- Adjusting the labor pool: This mechanism focuses on immigration measures that adjust the pool of foreign STEM workers (H-1B visa holders) allowed to work in the United States.
- Adjusting the workforce: this includes mechanisms (like those noted above in use by NASA and CDC) to recruit, retain, and promote STEM workers.

Historically, the most sweeping attempt to address STEM needs was the National Defense Education Act of 1958, passed in response to concerns about U.S. science education prompted by the Soviet Sputnik launches.

Conclusions

The data and observations discussed in this report suggest the following conclusions.

No Compelling Evidence of Current or Imminent Federal STEM Shortages

Our analysis found no compelling evidence of current or imminent shortages of STEM personnel in the federal workforce. Certain fields may develop shortages (e.g., rapidly growing sub-fields within information technology [IT]) and should be closely monitored. However, the downturn in the fortunes of the IT field after the Internet bubble burst makes such shortages less likely. In addition, STEM workers are not immune to employment variations over business cycles, although they tend to be less affected than other college graduates. In any case, for the general population, almost any shortfall in workers in any STEM field can be made up by changing H-1B Visa quotas and immigration policies.[4]

Likewise, we found no clear evidence of shortages in the federal STEM workforce. However, existing data are weak and do not support a comprehensive analysis. Some federal agencies believe there will be a problem in the near future as the number of STEM employees who are eligible for retirement increases, but indicators suggest that shortages, if any, will be less serious than many assert. This is principally because retirement eligibility does not translate automatically into retirement and because many federal workforce needs can be flexibly met through outsourcing to the private sector, thereby attaining access to the entire national labor market, and even the international labor market.

Our understanding of future federal STEM workforce requirements is limited by inadequate forecasts based on rough projections of current needs. The difficulty is further complicated by the federal government's growing propensity to contract out STEM work, which may decrease the in-house, civil service requirement. No adequate forecasts exist for this process, either.

We have found no comprehensive assessments of legislation or programs aimed at influencing the U.S. or federal STEM workforce. With respect to the two major types of federal mechanisms— (1) those aimed at filling the pipeline in educational and training facilities and (2) those aimed at shaping the workforce—we can conclude that the federal government mechanisms have focused primarily

---

[4] This point assumes that there is a supply of skilled workers elsewhere in the world. As economies outside the U.S. grow and become more developed, this assumption may no longer hold true.

on filling the pipeline, using mature institutions and programs that have been focused on this effort for decades. These pipeline-filling measures are now embedded in a mature institutional framework with implementing mechanisms refined by decades of experience. At the aggregate level, these measures have had some success addressing supply issues, including those affecting minorities and women. Federal agencies appear to have the statutory authority they need to conduct whatever innovative pipeline-filling programs are needed to address particular needs.

With respect to workforce-shaping mechanisms, the federal government has only recently begun to use these for STEM positions, and their use has varied widely by agency. Because most civil service STEM staffing is done at the agency level, there is not a great deal of precedence or experience using workforce management mechanisms across the entire federal STEM workforce. Cross-agency STEM workforce management initiatives require significant coordination that has proven difficult to engineer. However, there is no clear, widespread need for such programs. For example, retaining STEM workers does not seem to be a major problem for the federal government, implying that special retention mechanisms are probably needed sparingly and only in high demand sub-fields. However, there appear to be opportunities for workforce-shaping mechanisms in other areas, such as recruiting.

Given that many STEM graduates leave universities with sizable loan debt, some form of loan forgiveness or repayment as a recruiting mechanism could affect significant numbers of entering STEM workers. Whether such programs are widely needed is not clear, however.

A Clearer Picture of Federal STEM Workforce Requirements and Personnel Will Require Better Data

Agency perceptions of the federal STEM workforce suggest that it is an area of concern and that the federal government should monitor it. Doing so usefully in a timely way will require improved data. We identified deficiencies in the data that should be corrected to facilitate this process. Such improvements involve counting and describing both "spaces"—the requirements for workers with specific sets of skills, and "faces"—qualified persons actually filling the spaces.

Data on Spaces.[5] As commonly used in federal circles, the term "spaces" refers to requirements for STEM workers. The federal government needs to forecast the number of spaces it will require for all STEM specialties. Making such a forecast requires understanding evolving technology and changes in government roles. Data on future spaces should be consolidated within, or be accessible from, a central location. Relevant agencies might be required to develop and maintain forecasts for some years into the future, but not so many as to be beyond what could reasonably be anticipated. The federal government should develop a methodology for doing this forecasting and provide it to all departments and agencies. Additionally, attention should be paid to changes in the civil service/contractor mix in the federal STEM workforce, particularly if the current trend toward outsourcing continues.

Data on Faces. The data needed to adequately determine the ability of the national STEM workforce to supply the faces for filling the forecasted federal spaces are outlined in part in Chapter Three. Projection models for the national workforce are maintained by the Bureau of Labor Statistics. Other methods for filling STEM spaces (e.g., retraining workers into STEM specialties) should be considered in these models, as well as foreign workers and the output of standard education programs.

The broad patterns of STEM workforce requirements and availability reported here have emerged despite data that are not well suited to this purpose. Without better data, it will be difficult to undertake more-targeted investigations for particular STEM specialties,

---

[5] Our use of the "spaces" and "faces" terminology is not meant to assume that employers have fixed requirements for workers or that the definition of a qualified person is not subject to change. We presume that forecasts and data on requirements will want to take market and personnel flexibility into account to the maximum extent possible. So, for example, in the face of shortages, employers may redefine work and outsource some of it globally. Conversely, when there is an oversupply of highly skilled workers, employers may raise requirements for positions. We also note that forecasting STEM requirements is notoriously difficult, and to be useful, forecasts must be regularly updated and based on competent models.

particular agency employers, or particular geographic regions or demographic groups.

Next, we note the major data deficiencies that hamper a more firmly grounded and finely grained analysis than ours. The first set of deficiencies pertains to the broader U.S. STEM workforce, while the second pertains to the narrower federal STEM workforce. We include both because an understanding of the overall U.S. picture is important to the federal STEM workforce as well.

The U.S. STEM Workforce

The federal STEM workforce is a component of the U.S. STEM workforce, and in some ways is entirely reliant upon it. A look at U.S. STEM workforce data deficiencies is, therefore, necessary if one is to understand the federal STEM workforce.

Lack of Timeliness

- Publication of consistent data on major characteristics of the national STEM workforce often occurs more than two years after the fact.

Lack of Comparability

- Characterization of workers by area of formal education ("face" in our nomenclature) or job classification ("space") is inconsistent in the data.

Inconsistent Definitions

- Data from different sources feature varying definitions, time domains, and levels of disaggregation. This inconsistency also makes comparability more difficult to establish.
- Important data series have experienced changing definitions without reported crosswalks or even documentation.

Lack of Data

- Data on years to Ph.D. degree are not consistently available by discipline.

- Earnings, unemployment, underemployment, and other economic indicators of a shortage or surplus are not available consistently for the STEM workforce and its components.
- Data are unavailable on numbers of STEM workers in other than STEM spaces.
- There are no "flash" indicators[6] (available with, say, a one-quarter lag) of numbers of STEM students, proportion of foreign students, and numbers of STEM "spaces" in the federal government and private sector by major discipline and by selected critical sub-disciplines.

Federal STEM Workforce

Relevant data issues for the federal workforce are similar but not identical to those for the broader U.S. STEM workforce. As we have noted, OPM data on the federal workforce are much more timely than those available on the national workforce. They are also reasonably consistent across agencies. However, there are inconsistencies and gaps at the agency level and very little information on projections of future needs.

Inconsistent and Incomplete Data

- Consistent data are lacking on workforce retraining to meet STEM requirements.
- Current and historical demographic data on age, qualification level, and average age at retirement of STEM workers are incomplete.

---

[6] That is, there are no short turnaround indicators of pending shortages or surpluses that can quickly direct policymakers' attention to potential problem areas. These so-called flash indicators could provide early warning as quickly as three months after the fact. Additional in-depth data would then be gathered on these particular problem areas to decide whether the potential problems are serious or not. In the meantime, policy solutions would be at the ready. Such flash indicators might be developed for numbers of STEM students, proportions of foreign students, and numbers of STEM "spaces" in the federal government and private sector in selected critical subdisciplines.

- Few agencies maintain data on numbers and characteristics of the STEM workforce indirectly engaged through the A-76 mechanism or other outsourcing processes.
- Few agencies maintain forecasts of STEM worker requirements.

Lack of Data
- The data on STEM workers maintained by many agencies are no more detailed or complete than the data kept by the OPM.
- Data are unavailable on interagency mobility of STEM workers.
- There are no "flash" indicators of numbers of STEM students, proportion of foreign students, and numbers of STEM "spaces" in the federal government and private sector, by major discipline and selected critical sub-disciplines.
- There are no data available on the time interval between the government's decision to fill a STEM vacancy and its time of hiring a STEM worker to fill that vacancy. These data would shed light on the frequent claim that the federal government's long hiring time lags put it at a disadvantage relative to the private sector.

Some of these deficiencies are more damaging than others, depending on the particular focus of monitoring or analysis. Some are more easily corrected than others, depending on whether the cause of difficulty is at the source of the data or in the aggregation and reporting of the data. Processes for improving federal data statistics have been implemented in several areas in recent years. Establishing priorities, assigning responsibility, providing resources, and coordinating efforts could lead to similar improvements in the federal STEM workforce data.

These improvements that would result from these recommendations—when embodied in specific data with specified sources and methods—would permit statistical models to forecast STEM workforce trends in a comprehensive and timely manner and also permit comparisons of requirements (space forecasts) with personnel (face forecasts). Scientifically supportable policy decisions on STEM workforce mechanisms would be facilitated, as would informed training and career decisions by students and their advisors. Both personnel shortages and their attendant risks for the nation and personnel surpluses and their costs and disruptions for trained workers can thereby be reduced.

Acknowledgments

The authors thank the numerous federal officials who donated their time and shared their insights and information about federal STEM workforce issues during our many rounds of interviews. The National Aeronautics and Space Administration, the National Institutes of Health, the National Science Foundation, and the Departments of Agriculture, Energy, Defense, Homeland Security, and Transportation, as well as the Office of Management and Budget and the Office of Personnel Management were kind enough to permit us to interview members of their staffs.

We also thank Ellen Gadbois of the Office of Science and Data Policy of the Department of Health and Human Services, Michael Horrigan of the Bureau of Labor Statistics, and Mark Regets of the Science Resources Statistics Division of the National Science Foundation for their helpful comments on particular sections of the report.

We also thank our reviewers—Valerie Williams and Charlotte Kuh—for their careful and thorough reviews. Their comments and recommendations strengthened the report considerably.

As the authors did not accept all suggestions of interviewees and reviewers, we are solely responsible for any remaining errors of fact or interpretation.

Acronyms

ATSDR	Agency for Toxic Substances and Disease Registry
BEST	Building Engineering and Science Talent (partnership organization)
BLS	Bureau of Labor Statistics
CDC	Centers for Disease Control and Prevention
CFDA	*Catalog of Federal Domestic Assistance*
CS	Computer science
DHHS	Department of Health and Human Services
DHS	Department of Homeland Security
DMDC	Defense Data Management Center
DOC	Department of Commerce
DoD	Department of Defense
DOE	Department of Energy
DOL	Department of Labor
DOT	Department of Transportation
EPA	U.S. Environmental Protection Agency
EPD	Eisenhower Professional Development (grant)
ESEA	Elementary and Secondary Education Act of 1965
EIS	Epidemic Intelligence Service
FAA	Federal Aviation Administration

FBI	Federal Bureau of Investigation
FY	Fiscal year
GAO	U.S. General Accounting Office
GOCO	Government Owned, Contractor Operated
GSA	General Services Administration
HACU	Hispanic Association of Colleges and Universities
IT	Information technology
K–12	Kindergarten through grade 12
MSP	Math-Science Partnerships (Initiative)
NASA	National Aeronautics and Space Administration
NDEA	National Defense Education Act of 1958
NIH	National Institutes of Health
NSF	National Science Foundation
OMB	Office of Management and Budget
OPM	Office of Personnel Management
PHPS	Public Health Prevention Service
PMI	Presidential Management Intern
R&D	Research and development
RDT&E	Research, Development, Test, and Evaluation
STEM	Scientific, technical, engineering, and mathematics
U.S.C.	United States Code

CHAPTER ONE

Introduction

Recently, the size and adequacy of the federal workforce for carrying out scientific, technical, engineering, and mathematics (STEM)[1] activities have become areas of concern in many policy circles. Knowledgeable sources both inside and outside government have voiced fears that this workforce is aging and may soon face a dwindling labor pool, a concern that could be compounded by skill shortages in key areas as well as a growing proportion of non-U.S. citizens obtaining STEM degrees in the United States.

STEM Workforce Shortages: A Recurring Concern

Concerns about the federal STEM workforce[2] are variations on a recurring theme: a looming shortage of STEM workers in the United

---

[1] This workforce includes workers at all education levels who perform functions in these fields (e.g., computer technicians whose highest formal degree is a high school diploma, practicing engineers, medical doctors, and research scientists).

[2] This research does not address the specific composition or diversity of the federal STEM workforce, with the one exception of a brief look at the need for citizen versus non-citizen workers. It was developed based on available data and interviews with representatives from nine federal departments, agencies, or offices: the Departments of Homeland Security, Energy, Transportation, Health and Human Services (to include representatives from the Centers for Disease Control and Prevention and the Agency for Toxic Substances and Disease Registry), and Agriculture, the National Aeronautics and Space Administration, the National Science Foundation, the Office of Personnel Management, and the Office of Management and Budget.

States.[3] Knowledgeable and influential voices have sounded alarms over the adequacy of the numbers of STEM personnel graduating with STEM degrees and working in the United States. In view of an "unfolding crisis for U.S. science and technology," a task force of the National Science Board recommended in a May 2003 draft document for public comment a "national policy imperative" that "all stakeholders must mobilize and initiate efforts that increase the number of U.S. citizens pursuing science and engineering studies and careers."[4]

This is not the first such imperative. The earliest alarm, accompanied by concerns about kindergarten through grade 12 (K–12) education in the United States, led to landmark Federal legislation, the National Defense Education Act of 1958 (NDEA). The National Science and Technology Council sounded a similar warning in 2000, that "the potential shortage of skilled [STEM] workers could have devastating consequences for the future."[5, 6]

Sputnik was a triggering event for the NDEA, raising a red flag about the quality of American education and the need for a stronger federal role in improving STEM education in particular. More recent concerns about the STEM workforce have arisen for other reasons. One has been the rapid emergence of new high-technology fields such as information technology and genomics, fields that are deemed important for national competitiveness and security and that require technically trained workers. Another reason is the increasing technical

---

[3] This report addresses the issue of shortages from a broad STEM workforce perspective, and makes no claim to investigate the individual disciplinary issues of the workforce separately.

[4] From National Science Board, Committee on Education and Human Resources, Task Force on National Workforce Policies for Science and Engineering (2003). The final version of this document was released too late to be included in our study.

[5] National Science and Technology Council (2000).

[6] Other organizations—notably the American Academy for the Advancement of Science, the National Academy of Sciences, the Office of Technology Assessment, and the Government-University-Industry Research Roundtable—have also issued reports on the subject of STEM shortages. A number of studies from the National Academies have also explored related issues. These include National Research Council (2000b) and Institute of Medicine (1995). Many of the similar points on modeling and predicting are made in National Research Council (2000a) and, more recently, in National Research Council (2001).

demands of jobs that, even in traditional manufacturing and service industries, call for more highly technically trained workers. Other reasons for concern have focused on the education pipeline—the gradually decreasing numbers of M.S. and Ph.D. awards in several STEM fields, compared with the upcoming increasing requirements that have at times been predicted.

Another related concern, at the heart of the 2003 National Science Board draft report mentioned above, is the long-term declining proportion of U.S. citizens among STEM Ph.D.s granted by American institutions. This trend has potentially ominous implications for the future of American leadership in science and engineering, and additionally could pose difficulties for attempts to meet any increased demand for STEM professionals in national security and homeland security fields whose duties require security clearances.

The possible causes of these declines, if indeed they have continued after September 11, are diverse. Among the possible domestic causes are declining preparation for and interest in science careers in American K–12 classrooms; increasing attractiveness to potential graduate students of the immediate post–B.S.-degree job market during recent long economic expansions; increasing relative attractiveness of careers in medicine, law, business, and other professional fields that compete with science for bright American undergraduates; and lengthening graduate and post-doctorate training that raises the opportunity cost of preparation for entry into science careers.

Other possible causes for a declining proportion of citizens among STEM Ph.D.s could arise overseas. The causes might include an increase in the attractiveness of the American Ph.D. degree, leading in turn to increasing graduate school applications in the United States; a snowball effect from international professional networks established over decades, yielding a growing stream of top foreign applicants to work with their American mentors and friends; and an increased desire of foreign science students to live and work in the United States after their training.[7]

---

[7] Proposal of remedies for the declining relative participation of citizens in graduate STEM education would presumably benefit from prior identification of the actual causes, among all

Viewed broadly over the past half-century, evidence for the periodically anticipated shortages in the general STEM workforce has been hard to find. Still less evident so far have been indications of resulting national crises. Ironically, the closest thing to a crisis has perhaps been the distress of unemployed and underemployed engineers in the early 1970s, mathematicians and physicists in the 1990s, molecular and cellular biologists in the late 1990s, and Silicon Valley scientists and engineers thereafter. But these developments are the manifestations of surpluses, not shortages, in the STEM workforce. Conceptual consideration of what in fact constitutes a shortage and how to recognize one has not been much discussed in federal reports that warn of shortages.[8] Furthermore, those making a new assessment and forecast have not as a matter of course looked back to analyze what methodological or data improvements could have brought the previous forecasts closer to emerging reality.

Compounding these difficulties is the continually shifting definition of the STEM workforce, including whether it is best characterized by degree field or by current occupation or job. However the STEM workforce is defined, data to evaluate the numbers of STEM graduates and workers and available jobs for them have been inadequate for informed and timely policymaking. Finally, there has been little behavioral modeling and estimation of how these labor markets adjust to changes in supply and demand.[9]

---

of those that could be hypothesized. We are aware of little research in this specific direction and even less established knowledge. Yet, remedies are being confidently proposed. Confidence in the efficacy of these remedies and understanding of their possible unintended consequences would be born of focused research.

[8] Butz et al. (2003) propose alternative concepts of a STEM workforce shortage and provide an overview of the statistical evidence regarding each concept.

[9] The point is made in National Research Council, Office of Scientific and Engineering Personnel (2000b).

Conceptual Considerations of STEM Workforce Supply and Demand

Shortages and surpluses in a labor market arise from the interplay of supply and demand, including, in the modern global economy, international dimensions.

Supply

To understand the numbers and characteristics of STEM workers available to work for federal agencies, either in direct employment or through federal contractors, one must consider that this *supply* of workers depends, among other things, on three interacting factors:

- Restrictions placed on federal employees, e.g., U.S. citizenship
- Compensation, terms, and conditions of employment in competing non-federal jobs
- The time required for students and workers to adjust educational or vocational plans to meet market demands.

Consider, for example, a requirement with a very short time horizon of several months. Few students in majors other than that stipulated by the requirement can switch to the appropriate STEM fields and then graduate within several months. Moreover, most current STEM workers are already employed and will not change jobs and locations that quickly, few federal jobs can be shifted to contractors, and non-U.S. citizens cannot be drawn into federal employment because they are precluded from that employment by law. In such a short period, therefore, the federal government (and many other employers) cannot add significantly to its STEM workforce.

Only in an extreme emergency would the federal government need to bring on board a substantial number of STEM workers in such a short time. With a more realistic time horizon of several years, worker availability becomes more elastic. Some students nearing their terminal degrees can convert to a STEM field, most STEM workers otherwise employed can consider shifting to direct federal or contract employment, and more radically, federal hiring restrictions could be loosened to increase the supply of qualified workers. In these ways, substantially more STEM workers could be drawn to direct or contract government employment over this medium-run period of several years.

Finally, with a time horizon of a decade or more, most high school students and nearly all more advanced students who choose a STEM career will attain terminal degrees and be potentially available for government employment. Furthermore, labor market adjustments involving already employed workers who decide to change jobs or occupations will be complete over this long run.

Whatever the length of time allowed for adjustment of education pipelines and the labor market, the supply of STEM workers to the government will increase as the government's legal and administrative restrictions on hiring decrease. Educational and private-sector employers are the government's principal competition in the STEM labor market.[10] As they recruit workers, these employers are subject to the same range of time-dependent student and worker responsiveness as is the government. Beyond this time dimension, however, most private employers are subject to fewer legal and administrative restrictions on the worker pool from which they can hire. The most significant difference is private organizations' ability to hire non-citizens.

If the need for government STEM workers were sufficiently serious, the government might loosen these restrictions, thereby opening federal jobs to new pools of potential applicants. For example, opening more job positions to contractors who are subject to fewer hiring restrictions would extend the government's employment reach further into the private-sector labor market. More radically, loosening the citizenship requirement for federal employment would widen the pool of potential STEM workers still further, not only to those foreign nationals now studying and working in the United Stated but also to others who might immigrate in response to this opportunity. Loosening immigration restrictions on foreign students, scientists,

---

[10] Overseas foreign employers also compete for American STEM workers, but currently to a much lesser extent.

and engineers would facilitate this immigration, expanding the pool still further.[11]

The federal government can also increase the supply of STEM workers by helping to improve the quality of STEM education in K–12 and beyond, and by reducing the cost to students of attaining STEM degrees. The first action can interest more pupils in science careers, while the second action—often through fellowships—can reduce their cost of preparing for these careers.

These considerations on the workforce *supply* side lead to two important conclusions: First, the potential supply of STEM workers to the federal government is considerably larger than might at first appear, particularly if the time horizon for adjustment is long. Second, the federal government can influence this supply of STEM workers.

Of course, the numbers and characteristics of workers actually employed by the federal government, either directly or on contract, depend not only on labor supply but also on the terms and conditions of such employment: compensation, working conditions, job challenge and satisfaction, training and mobility opportunities, retirement benefits, and such. These are the expressions of the government's *demand* for STEM workers. It is largely these job characteristics that induce some or many of the existing eligible STEM workers to work for the government instead of elsewhere. Over a long time horizon, these same job characteristics can influence even the size of the total STEM workforce, by inducing students to choose STEM careers.[12] However, this full response will occur only if the govern-

---

[11] These three employment liberalizations would have broader political, legal, and economic ramifications than simply expanding the government workforce; we note here only this one effect in order to clarify the range of potentially available options for increasing federal STEM employment.

[12] In particular, these job characteristics can induce changes in the supply of workers in occupations in which the federal government is a prominent enough employer that its hiring actions and intentions influence the terms and conditions that other employers must offer to compete. In these occupations, the federal government can ultimately affect the relative attractiveness of them, market-wide. In this situation, not only some existing STEM workers can be expected to react to a change in government employment conditions, but also some students who alter their career plans accordingly.

ment is successful in signaling its job characteristics in such a way that students (and their advisers) perceive the characteristics to persist over the years until the students complete their schooling and enjoy the jobs for which they prepared.

Accordingly, advertising that the government has a requirement for some number of STEM workers cannot be expected to bring to the employment interview as many high-quality potential employees as advertising that compensation, working conditions, and the like are more than competitive with private industry and will remain so for a long time. The latter strategy, while more expensive, can be expected to produce results, whether for one scientific subspecialty or across the STEM spectrum.

A frequent policy response to a perceived shortage of STEM workers has been to increase or extend financial support for students. As we have seen, this action can be expected to increase the supply of STEM workers after some years. Attention to the demand side—for example, making sure more job slots with improved compensation and working conditions will be available when the graduating scientists and engineers come on line—is much less common.[13] When the interest is in STEM employment for a particular employer, like the federal government, it may well be more efficient to work on the demand side by improving compensation and working conditions than on the supply side by increasing overall numbers available to any employer, only some of whom will choose federal jobs.

Demand

When we talk about the need for a STEM workforce, we are necessarily measuring that need against some concept of demand or "requirement." At the level of an agency of the federal government, a competent and correctly sized STEM workforce is necessary to accomplish certain goals (e.g., to put a man on the moon required cer-

---

[13] Particular agencies faced with particular staff shortages do sometimes request and receive permission to improve compensation and conditions, but the federal agencies charged with the health of the overall science and engineering enterprise tend to ignore this "pull" of jobs in favor of increasing the "push" on career choice and training.

tain specialties of scientists, technicians, engineers, and mathematicians in certain numbers). Whether the STEM workforces of the nation and the federal government are large enough, and of the right composition, will depend upon the national goals they will work to achieve and upon their efficiency in achieving them.[14] For the nation, these goals are dynamic and not centrally managed, determined, or even knowable. For the federal government, more specificity exists, but here again the requirements are dynamic and difficult to pin down. In fact, when speaking of organizations, our concept of what is needed will depend (among other things) on our definition of the word "requirement"—whether that means what is actually needed to address the organization's STEM challenges or what managers say is needed. This will be addressed in Chapter Three, where we focus on the latter definition and discuss how it is connected to the former. Furthermore, concepts of sufficiency often depend on indirect metrics such as economic indicators (e.g., unemployment, salary, retention rates).

The International Dimension

There is one more important dimension of the context in which STEM labor markets operate that needs to be considered: the global supply and demand for STEM workers. As the U.S. H-1B visa programs have demonstrated in the past decade, when domestic supplies of certain skills are insufficient, there is a world market that might fill certain needs, but worldwide demand could also shut off the flow of certain skilled workers, and draw U.S. citizens to work in other nations. Although this scenario does not seem to be an immediate concern, two examples are instructive. First, security restrictions affecting foreign STEM students and workers wishing to come to the United States could have unforeseen consequences on the supply of special-

---

[14] In Chapter Two, we will look at the national STEM workforce, and in Chapter Three we will consider the federal STEM workforce and how it overlaps with that of the nation. As a basis for comparison, as of December 2002, there were 276,581 STEM workers out of 1,843,738 total workers in the federal civil service, or 15 percent of the federal workforce. Note that this includes many non–graduate-degree holders.

ists in these fields, an important component of the national STEM workforce. On the other hand, the growth of computer science and information technology fields abroad has shifted some IT business oversees, and with it some STEM workers who might otherwise do federal government work. Both affect the nation's ability to meet the STEM requirement. Within this national and international context, this report considers the adequacy of the STEM workforce for the requirements of the federal government.

Purpose and Organization of This Report

The failure of previously anticipated crises in the STEM workforce to occur is not grounds for complacency. The implications of a shortage of skills critical to U.S. growth, competitiveness, and security are serious, probably more so now than in recent decades, as are the implications of the continuing low entry of female and minority students into many STEM fields, noted particularly in the National Science and Technology Council (2000) and National Science Board (2003) reports. These implications justify periodic examinations of the nature and sources of the production of scientists, technical workers, engineers, and mathematicians in the United States.

This report constitutes such an examination.[15] Some experts fear that the federal government is facing a shortage of STEM workers. Managers and other decision makers in federal agencies point to high proportions of retirement age workers in the current federal workforce and of non-citizens among recent STEM graduates who will form the future workforce. Both trends together could portend a

---

[15] As we define it, the U.S. STEM workforce consists of people with certificates and degrees from trade schools, community colleges, universities, and graduate programs. Ph.D.s are a critical portion of this workforce but not the only portion. In important respects, the relative importance of the other portions may be growing. And of course, beyond this broad workforce, a basic level of scientific and technical understanding is important for all the nation's citizens. Perceived inadequacy of such understanding has also caused concern for decades, but it is beyond the scope of this study, except insofar as it affects the quantity and quality of the STEM workforce down the line.

possible shortage of U.S. citizen scientists and engineers, even as defense and homeland security concerns are accelerating the government's requirements.

Chapter Two examines the national STEM workforce to elucidate STEM workers' availability for federal employment, either directly as government employees or indirectly as contract workers. The chapter relies on national-level statistical data from the Science Resources Statistics Division of the National Science Foundation, the Bureau of Labor Statistics, U.S. Census Bureau, National Academies of Sciences, numerous professional associations, and other sources. Chapter Three provides analysis of data from federal agencies to identify trends in the numbers and characteristics of STEM workers directly employed by the federal government. Nearly as many STEM workers on government projects are employed by private contractors as by the government itself, but these workers cannot be readily identified, counted, or described using existing data. Chapter Three includes such evidence as exists on the size of this contract workforce. The chapter relies on data provided by federal departments and agencies that employ large numbers of STEM workers, directly or on contract, and data provided by the Office of Personnel Management. This report's authors interviewed managers in several of these agencies, whose perceptions and expectations of STEM personnel needs and availability informed the authors' use of agency numbers.[16]

Chapter Four describes the key federal mechanisms in use—both legislative and programmatic at the agency level—to affect STEM education and the STEM workforce, in order to identify those mechanisms that might be applicable in today's shifting economic, international, and security contexts. For this chapter, we constructed a legislative and programmatic history of federal efforts to improve and extend STEM education and to influence the job choice of STEM workers. We also reviewed subsequent evaluation studies.

---

[16] Readers who are primarily interested in our analysis of the federal STEM workforce may wish to skip Chapter Two, the background chapter on the broader issues surrounding the U.S. STEM workforce, and proceed directly to Chapter Three.

Chapter Five draws conclusions supported by the available data and also identifies particular data additions and improvements that would provide policymakers, employers, and students with a sounder basis for decision making in the future.

The U.S. STEM Workforce

If the federal government does face current or looming shortages of STEM workers, these trends might be mirrored at the national level. Therefore, the first stage of our analysis examines the size and characteristics of the U.S. STEM workforce, including unemployment, salary trends, and other economic indicators.[1] This chapter presents the results of that analysis.

First, we discuss trends in size and growth of the U.S. STEM workforce. Next, we describe and analyze the numbers and characteristics of STEM students and new graduates, as they are likely the principal source of prospective growth in the pool of STEM workers

---

[1] Common usage makes no clear distinction between the nouns "prediction," "forecast," and "projection." However, in economics, demography, and statistics, they have distinct meanings. A *prediction* is an unconditional statement about a phenomenon not yet observed. A *forecast* is a statement (about a phenomenon not yet observed) that is meant to hold under certain explicit conditions. A *projection* is a statement (about a phenomenon not yet observed) based entirely on current and past instances of the phenomenon. Hence, if we *predict* a shortage of STEM workers in five years, we mean either that a shortage is expected, or that we have previously predicted the other factors that will determine a shortage and derived our workforce prediction accordingly. The prediction is unconditional and is falsified if there is no shortage, no matter why. Alternatively, we may *forecast* a shortage of STEM workers in five years, conditional on increasing homeland security requirements and declining STEM training by U.S. students. If either of these conditions does not occur, our forecast does not apply. Finally, we may *project* a shortage of STEM workers based only on underlying extrapolations of student cohort sizes and recent trends in STEM enrollment, along with extrapolation of recent changes in numbers of slots for STEM workers in the economy. We think that what most observers intend when they make statements about the future STEM workforce, is forecasts, even though the observers are frequently imprecise about the underlying conditions. Accordingly, we use the term "forecast" in this report, except where otherwise indicated.

available to the federal government in the foreseeable future. Moreover, most policy and program measures aimed at increasing the STEM workforce have focused in one way or another on students. We then examine trends in non-U.S. employees in this workforce. Finally, we examine economic indicators that might indicate whether there are shortages or surpluses of STEM workers in the United States.

U.S. citizens constitute the pool from which all federal STEM employees can be recruited without changes in current laws and regulations. When augmented by new citizen graduates in STEM fields, this more-comprehensive (but not necessarily larger)[2] workforce constitutes the pool of federal STEM employees in the long run, i.e., over a decade or more. When augmented still further by non-citizens, this comprehensive workforce constitutes the pool of STEM workers available to federal agencies through either direct or contract employment.[3] This larger workforce is, indeed, the national STEM workforce from which all employers, public and private, draw.

U.S. STEM Workforce Data

The Science Resources Statistics Division of the National Science Foundation collects and publishes most available statistics on the nation's STEM students and workers. This chapter is based on these statistics, along with other data from the U.S. Census Bureau, the U.S. Bureau of Labor Statistics, the National Research Council, the (former) Office of Technology Assessment, several scientific associations, and research studies.

---

[2] The number of retirements could exceed the number of new STEM entrants in some periods, causing a decline in total STEM employment. However, federal actions to increase STEM employment can be expected to raise the total above what it would have been, particularly as such actions would likely induce some existing federal workers to stay in their jobs.

[3] The largest possible pool, including foreign students and STEM workers now precluded from immigrating, is beyond the scope of this report.

Unfortunately, the uneven detail, varying definitions, and inconsistent time periods in the available data complicate the analyst's task and challenge the reader. As of early 2003, when our analysis was conducted, data more recent than 1999 or 2000 were generally not yet published, making it difficult to assess the current STEM workforce given the major changes in the economic and policy environments since then. The picture of the nation's STEM workforce that emerges is nevertheless reasonably coherent. We return to this issue in Chapter Five, where we consider additions and improvements to the nation's STEM workforce statistics that would provide a more complete and more timely picture of both national and federal employment.

Trends in the Size of the U.S. STEM Workforce

Figure 2.1 shows that employment in STEM occupations in the United States grew by about 80 percent between 1980 and 1999.[4] Although definitional changes cloud direct comparisons between 1980–1992 and 1993–1999, one sees here little or no evidence of a declining workforce.[5]

---

[4] This is the first of many places in this report where more-recent data are sorely missed. Without such data, it is difficult to say whether trends (such as those illustrated in Figure 2.1) have continued. To the extent that the recent past is the firmest basis for discerning the near future, such discernment is now too easily left to speculation based on anecdote, parochial impressions, and organizational self-interest.

[5] Data for 1980 through 1992 are from the 1993 *Science and Engineering Indicators* (National Science Board, 1993). These data represent the total number of scientists and engineers, excluding social scientists, employed in industry for those years. Information on the highest degree level for those counted in this total was not available. Data for 1993 through 1999 are from the 2002 Indicators (National Science Board, 2002a and 2002b). These data represent the total number of individuals employed in STEM occupations in business and industry for those years, including those in the social sciences, who held at least a bachelor's degree. In both cases, the data exclude those individuals performing STEM-related functions whose occupations are not categorized as "STEM" and individuals holding degrees from foreign countries now holding STEM jobs in the United States. Data for the most-recent years also exclude individuals in STEM jobs without bachelor's degrees. For these reasons, the more-recent data likely underestimate the actual number of individuals employed in STEM occupations during these years. In particular, changes between 1992 and 1993 indi-

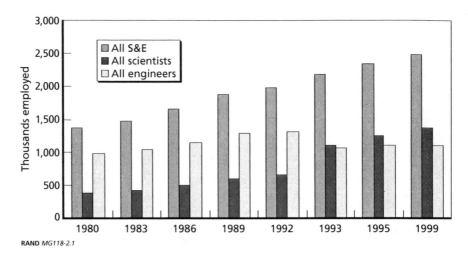

RAND *MG118-2.1*

SOURCES: National Science Board, 2002b, Appendix Tables 2-15 through 2-18; National Science Board, 1993, Table 3.1.

NOTE: In regard to the 1995 figures, data published in the 2002 indicators were identical for the years 1995 and 1997, making the year to which the data applied ambiguous. Conversations with National Science Foundation staff were not able to clear up this ambiguity.

Figure 2.1—Employment in STEM Occupations

How this number of STEM workers has been changing compared with total employment can be more clearly seen in Figure 2.2, which shows the changes over successive three-year periods between surveys.[6] The height of each bar represents the addition (or subtraction) of jobs from one period to the next. Note that the growth of jobs in both science and engineering was accelerating during the 1980s, with engineering jobs growing more rapidly than science jobs. Between 1989 and 1992, however, the growth in both series slowed, dropping nearly to zero growth for engineers.

---

cated in the figure may be spurious. Detailed information as to which occupations qualified as "STEM" and whether these categories remained constant over the time period of the data was not available.

[6] For each bar, the number of individuals employed in the earlier year was subtracted from the number employed in the later year to obtain the change across the time period.

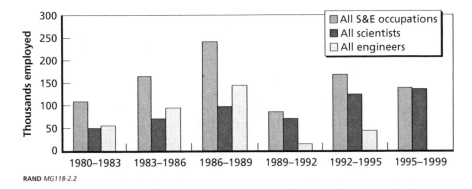

RAND MG118-2.2

SOURCES: National Science Board, 2002b, Appendix Tables 2-15 through 2-18; National Science Board, 1993, Table 3.1.

Figure 2.2—Changes in STEM Employment, 1980–1999

Unfortunately, we cannot locate data on the sources of the changes represented in Figure 2.2. To understand these sources would require data on numbers of persons leaving the ranks of the STEM workforce (due to job change to a non-STEM position, retirement, emigration, or death) and, separately, numbers of persons entering the STEM workforce (due to labor market entry after graduation, job change, or immigration). Such "gross flows" data would be particularly useful for identifying possible patterns of unusually large STEM worker entry in some periods that might produce predictably large declines on into the future as these workers retire. Unfortunately, we cannot locate such gross flows data for the nation's STEM workforce, much less for its disciplinary or occupational components.[7]

---

[7] Gross flows can reportedly be estimated from the U.S. Department of Labor Bureau of Labor Statistics Current Population Survey data, but we have not pursued this possibility (Horrigan, 2003).

Entrants to the STEM Workforce

Unless immigration restrictions are significantly relaxed, the principal source of new STEM workers will continue to be technically trained graduates of schools in the United States. Figure 2.3 shows that these numbers have generally increased between 1966 and 1998. Two hundred thousand more STEM bachelor's degrees were awarded in 1999 than in 1966, a doubling of the number of degrees. While the numbers of M.S. and Ph.D. degrees also approximately doubled, their numerical increases have been much less than those of bachelor's degrees. As a consequence, the proportion of persons attaining a bachelor's degree who also complete a Ph.D. has fallen substantially.

Figure 2.4 views STEM degree production from another angle, the relative numbers of degrees awarded in all fields at each level. Thirty-five percent of bachelor's degrees awarded in 1966 were in STEM fields. After a slow decline, 32 percent were in STEM fields

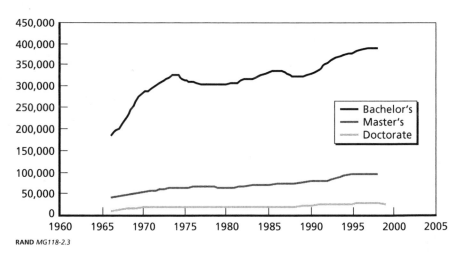

RAND MG118-2.3

SOURCES: National Science Foundation, 1996, Appendix Tables C-5, C-12, and C-19; National Science Board, 2002b, Tables 2-16, 2-22, and 2-24.

NOTE: The master's degrees do not include master of social work (MSW) degrees.

Figure 2.3—Total STEM Degrees Conferred, 1966–1998

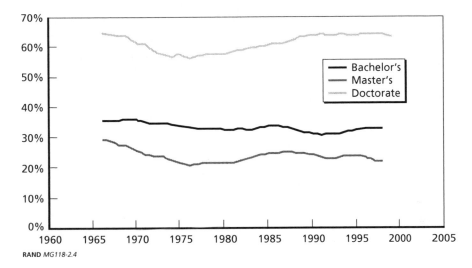

SOURCES: National Science Foundation, 1996; National Science Board, 2002a and 2002b.

Figure 2.4—Proportion of Degrees Conferred in STEM Fields, 1966–1998

33 years later. In the decade after 1966, this ratio declined more precipitously for master's degrees. STEM Ph.D.s as a proportion of all doctorates[8] ended the 33-year period about where they began. The long-term decline in the probabilities that a bachelor's or master's degree are in a STEM field appears independent of business cycles,[9] and neither of the two series leads the Ph.D. series predictably, as one would expect if students are making or changing their plans on the basis of short-run economic activity.

---

[8] The term "doctorate" or "doctoral degree" as used here and elsewhere in this report, refers to research doctorates only unless otherwise stipulated. "Doctorate" is used in this way in order to properly reflect how the term is used in the source documents. According to the NSF *Survey of Earned Doctorates, Methodology Report 2000–2001* (available at http://www.nsf.gov/sbe/srs/ssed/start.htm as of January 2004), an annual census and survey of new recipients of research doctorates from U.S. institutions, "While typically a Ph.D., the research doctorate is a doctoral degree that (1) requires the completion of a dissertation or equivalent project of original work (e.g., musical composition, etc.) and (2) is not exclusively intended as a degree for the practice of a profession. Degrees such as Psy.D., D.Min., Pharm.D., M.D., etc. are not included. Ed.D.s are included if they are research oriented."

[9] Economic recessions over this period occurred in 1970–1971, 1980–1982, and 1992.

Figures 2.5, 2.6, and 2.7 show changes by degree field for bachelor's, master's, and doctorate degrees from 1975 to 1998. Of the 13 fields represented, only biological and agricultural science, computer science, electrical engineering, and psychology show increasing bachelor's degree production over the period. Bachelor's degrees in mathematics, the physical sciences, and most engineering fields have stayed steady or declined.

At the master's level among the same 13 fields, computer science, electrical and mechanical engineering, psychology, and the

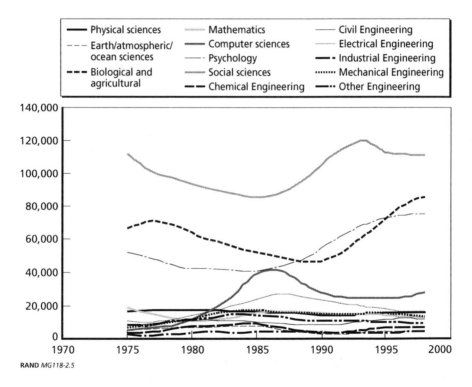

SOURCE: National Science Board, 2002b, Appendix Table 2-16.

Figure 2.5—Bachelor's Degrees for Sub-STEM Fields, Both Sexes, Earned at U.S. Institutions (U.S. and Foreign Students)

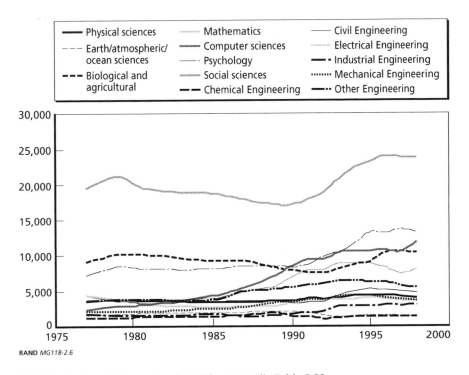

—— Physical sciences	⋯⋯ Mathematics	—— Civil Engineering
––– Earth/atmospheric/ ocean sciences	══ Computer sciences	⋯⋯⋯ Electrical Engineering
	—·— Psychology	—·— Industrial Engineering
■■■ Biological and agricultural	▓▓▓ Social sciences	⋯⋯⋯ Mechanical Engineering
	—— Chemical Engineering	—⋯ Other Engineering

RAND *MG118-2.6*

SOURCE: National Science Board, 2002b, Appendix Table 2-22.

Figure 2.6—Master's Degrees for Sub-STEM Fields, Both Sexes, Earned at U.S. Institutions (U.S. and Foreign Students)

social sciences saw an increase in the number of graduates over the indicated years. Among Ph.D.s, some 60 percent more biological and agricultural science degrees were granted in 1998 than in 1970. Only psychology and computer science experienced as large a percentage increase, the latter field having starting from a low level of graduates in 1970. The number of electrical engineering and mathematics Ph.D.s also increased, although not as rapidly as in other fields.

Across the three levels of degrees, biological and agricultural sciences have experienced the largest and steadiest increases in degrees granted, followed by computer science and psychology. Mathematics

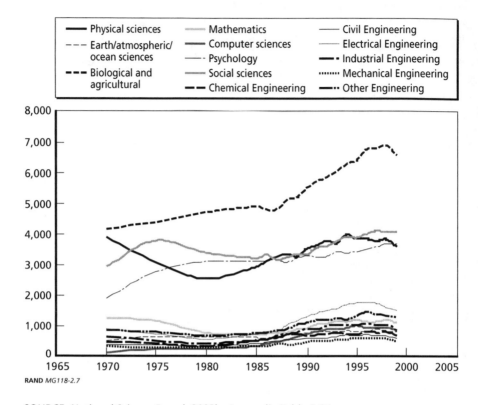

SOURCE: National Science Board, 2002b, Appendix Table 2-24.

Figure 2.7—Doctorate Degrees for Sub-STEM Fields, Both Sexes, Earned at U.S. Institutions (U.S. and Foreign Students)

and physical science degrees have increased the least, when they have increased at all.[10]

---

[10] It is important to note that in 1970 computer science was just being recognized as a discipline. At the time, there were very few computer science (CS) departments, so there were almost no CS degrees. Instead, CS was studied in mathematics or statistics departments. Hence, the increase in computer science degrees can be attributed in some measure to the difference in the number of computer science departments over the years. There were Ph.D. computer scientists earlier than 1970, but their Ph.D.s were in mathematics or statistics. Indeed, the less-rapid growth in math and electrical engineering may be because CS students increasingly had their own department to enroll in.

Non-Citizens Among STEM Graduates

Where federal employment is concerned, interest in Ph.D. production extends beyond the total numbers to a concern about relative growth of citizens and non-citizens holding doctoral degrees in the STEM workforce. Accordingly, Figure 2.8 shows total Ph.D.s and STEM Ph.D.s from 1986 to 1999, as well as Ph.D.s and STEM Ph.D.s for citizens and non-citizens as proportions of the totals. While STEM degree production has risen less rapidly than total degree production, both turned down in 1999, the most-recent reported year.[11] Likewise, the proportion of non-citizens among STEM Ph.D. recipients did not increase by as much over the period as the

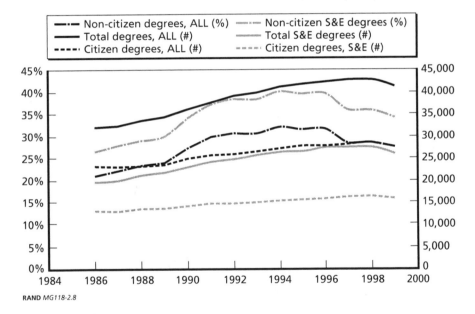

RAND *MG118-2.8*

SOURCE: National Science Board, 2002b, Appendix Table 2-26.

Figure 2.8—Share of Total and STEM Doctoral Degrees Earned by Citizens and Non-Citizens in the United States

---

[11] Here, the lack of more-recent data is particularly debilitating.

proportion of non-citizens among all Ph.D. recipients. Therefore, neither the number of Ph.D.s awarded nor the proportion of Ph.D.s awarded to non-citizens has grown as much in STEM fields as in other fields, but each has grown nevertheless.

Earnings and Unemployment of STEM Workers

It is in the labor market that the demand for workers, whether from the federal government or elsewhere, and the supply of workers, whether citizens or not, come together. When the demand for a particular type of worker is increasing relative to the supply, earnings for those workers can be expected to rise while their unemployment rate falls. Conversely, if demand growth is insufficient to absorb an increasing supply of workers, earnings will fall while unemployment rises. Hence, labor market conditions, as indicated by earnings and unemployment, provide useful indicators of shortages or surpluses in the labor market. Available data on these measures for scientists and engineers are sketchy, but they are consistent.

Figure 2.9 compares an estimate of annualized earnings for Ph.D.s (all Ph.D.s are included in this measure, not just STEM Ph.D.s)[12] with earnings of professional degree holders (e.g., MDs, JDs, MBAs).[13] Professional degree holders earn more at nearly every

---

[12] These highly aggregated data cannot reveal salary trends for just the STEM workforce, much less for particular disciplines and sub-disciplines that may have experienced unusual salary growth or decline. For comparison purposes, about 60 percent of Ph.D. degree holders were in STEM fields in the period covered by these data.

[13] Called a "synthetic estimate of work life earnings" by the U.S. Census Bureau, this measure calculates for the 1997–1999 period the annual earnings of persons in each indicated age range. A young person today might interpret the lines connecting these age points as the expected career profile of annual earnings on into his or her future. That interpretation requires several strong assumptions. An alternative measure of the career earnings profile would report annual earnings of the same group of people as they age over the years. As those data must necessarily refer entirely to the past, even to the deep past when the group of people was young, they also are a flawed proxy for looking at the future. However, lacking real data about the future, people and organizations use information about the past and present to make decisions, including career decisions.

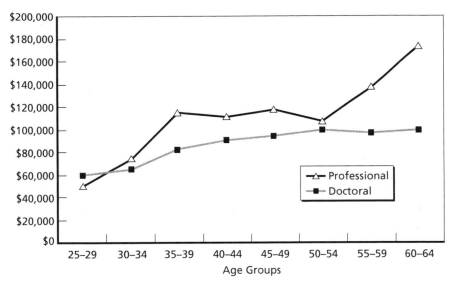

RAND *MG118-2.9*

SOURCE: Day and Newburger, 2002, p. 10.

Figure 2.9—Synthetic Estimates of Annual Work Life Earnings

age and considerably more over an entire career, as measured by the summed difference between the lines. This is no surprise.

For the purpose of our analysis, we would be better served had these earnings estimates been calculated separately for the STEM workforce a decade or so earlier and then repeated. Such a comparison would then reveal whether the professional degree premium is falling—that is, whether the relative attractiveness of a STEM career is rising, indicating unsatisfied demand. Alas, this measure is not yet separately available for STEM degree holders.[14] Still, the data at hand give no indication of the kind of earnings premiums for scientists and

---

[14] The American Association for the Advancement of Science recently completed a salary survey in the life sciences, but too late for a discussion of it to be included in this report. See http://recruit.sciencemag.org/feature/salsurvey/salarysurvey.htm. A separate comparison of changes over the 1982–2002 period can be made with Current Population Survey data, but was beyond the analytic scope of this analysis.

engineers that would signal the existence of a shortage of STEM workers.

Unemployment rates are another indicator of market conditions. Rates that are falling or that are lower than in alternative occupations also suggest unsatisfied demand. Unemployment rates are available and plotted in Figure 2.10 for chemists, recent mathematics Ph.D.s, and recent biomedical Ph.D.s.[15] Although not fully comparable by population or time period, the three rates, when compared with the overall U.S. unemployment rate, suggest a general increase

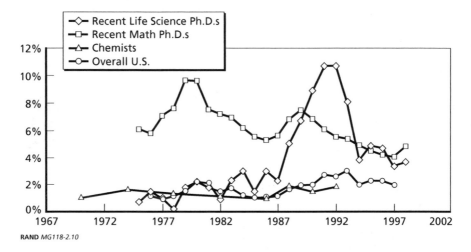

RAND MG118-2.10

SOURCES: National Research Council, 1998; Heylin, 1999 and 2000; Loftsgaarden, Maxwell, and Priestley, 2002; and Bureau of Labor Statistics, n.d.

NOTE: "Recent" Ph.D.s in Math is defined as those having received or expecting their degree within one year of the survey. "Recent" Ph.D.s in the Life Sciences is defined as those having received their degree within ten years of the survey and is a weighted average of the cohort data reported in the cited source. Unemployment data was gathered from Chemistry Ph.D.s, regardless of when they earned their degree.

Figure 2.10—Unemployment Rates of U.S. Workers Overall and Workers in Selected STEM Field

---

[15] The American Mathematical Society and American Chemical Association publish more extensive data (including unemployment rates) on their members than do most other STEM communities.

or leveling in STEM employment during the 1990s, while the general unemployment rate was falling substantially. Rising unemployment in one sector, while the overall economy is doing well, is a strong indicator of developing surpluses of workers, not shortages.

The data in Figure 2.11 are particularly revealing. Here, the proportions of STEM workers involuntarily employed out of their field of training because full-time work in their field was not available can be followed over the course of the 1990s. It can also be compared with the same proportion of non-STEM workers (the second-from-the-right bar in each set). Note first that this "underemployment rate" is considerably higher for social scientists, life scientists, and physical scientists in every year than for the other three groups, including the rate for non-STEM workers. Note second that for the first three groups the rates stayed high through 1997, even as the

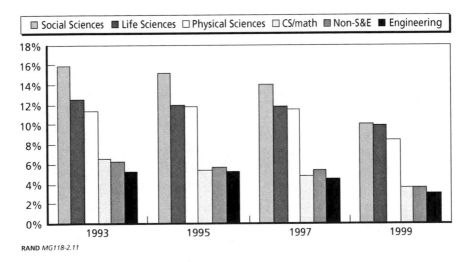

RAND MG118-2.11

SOURCE: Scientist and Engineers Statistical Data System (SESTAT), "SESTAT Detailed Statistical Tables," 1993–1999 (available at http://srsstats.sbe.nsf.gov/).

NOTE: "Rate" is defined as the percentage of workers who reported working part time or in an area not related to their highest degree exclusively because suitable full-time work in their field was not available.

Figure 2.11—Involuntary Out-of-Field Employment Rates Across Degree Fields

non-STEM underemployment rate was falling. Only the "under-employment rate" for engineers has been lower than that for non-STEM workers in every year.[16] Hence, neither earnings patterns nor unemployment and underemployment patterns indicate a STEM worker shortage in the available data. Altogether, the data in Figures 2.9, 2.10, and 2.11 do not portray the kind of vigorous employment and earnings prospects that would be expected to draw increasing numbers of bright and informed young people into STEM fields.[17]

Is There a National Shortfall of STEM Workers?

Despite recurring concerns about potential shortages of STEM personnel in the U.S. workforce, particularly in engineering and information technology, we do not find evidence that such shortages have existed at least since 1990 or that they are on the horizon.

If there were shortages of STEM workers, we would expect to observe low levels of unemployment and rising wages for STEM workers. Examining earning patterns and employment patterns for STEM workers, we find no patterns that are consistent with a shortage of STEM workers. The statistics do not portray the kinds of vigorous earnings and employment prospects that would be expected to draw increasing numbers of workers into STEM fields.

Likewise, "underemployment patterns"—indications of STEM workers involuntarily working out of their fields—suggest that the underemployment rates of STEM workers are relatively high compared with those of non-STEM workers. Engineering is an exception—its underemployment rate historically has been lower than for non-STEM workers.

---

[16] The STEM workers counted in Figure 2.11 include all those whose highest degree is in a STEM field and persons holding a non-STEM degree who were employed in a STEM occupation.

[17] The considerable variety of skills required within many occupations means that shortages (or surpluses) can occur in workforces in the upper part of the earnings distribution that are not reflected in median earnings measures for an occupation. These distinctions are difficult to discern in the available data.

There are also concerns about the high proportion of non-citizens earning STEM degrees in the United States. This trend was up at least between 1970 and the mid-1990s. More recently in the half decade before 2000, this proportion leveled off. Overall, the growth of non-citizen STEM Ph.D.s granted by U.S. institutions was proportionally less than the growth of non-citizen non-STEM Ph.D.s granted by U.S. institutions.

Based on these indicators, we find neither an inadequate supply of STEM workers to supply the nation's current needs, nor indications of shortages of STEM workers in the foreseeable future. While it may be argued that any possibility of shortages must be met by accelerating the supply, the cost to young people of emerging from years of training into labor markets struggling with worker surpluses should also be considered. Over the past half century, the latter situation has occurred much more frequently than the former.[18]

---

[18] Note that this statement does not claim that labor market conditions have not been generally good for STEM workers. Rather, it points out that the data presented in this report indicate periodic worker surpluses and a softening of the employment market for important elements of the STEM workforce.

CHAPTER THREE

The Federal STEM Workforce

In this chapter, we look more closely at the federal STEM workforce. We report results from a series of interviews with federal agencies, examine the available data, and discuss the requirements for a comprehensive analysis of the workforce. We interviewed research managers at selected federal agencies, including the National Aeronautics and Space Administration (NASA), the National Institutes of Health (NIH), the Departments of Agriculture, Defense, Energy, Homeland Security, and Transportation, as well as the Office of Management and Budget (OMB), and the Office of Personnel Management.

The interviews sought answers to three primary questions:

- What STEM workforce issues do federal managers encounter, and what do they think are the causes of these issues?
- What policies and data-gathering processes are in place to help address these issues?
- What can available data tell us about the issues identified by federal managers?

In the discussion that follows, we provide an overview of the composition of the federal STEM workforce, assess what data would be needed to conduct a comprehensive assessment of its size and adequacy, examine what the available data can tell us, and finally offer our observations on the federal STEM workforce's current status.

Overview of the Federal STEM Workforce

As we have stated, the federal STEM workforce includes both civil service and contract employees.[1] Note that the contract workforce includes the workforce of private-sector companies that provide goods and services to the government (e.g., aircraft for the military or buildings for the General Services Administration [GSA]). With respect to recruiting and maintaining a workforce with appropriate skills and talents, this contract workforce makes up a very large portion of the federal STEM workforce and is in many ways indistinguishable from the national STEM workforce.[2] This implies that the observations in Chapter Two about the sufficiency of STEM workers nationally may apply to problems of recruiting and retention in this contract portion of the federal workforce as well.

It is important to note that although we often refer to the federal "STEM workforce" in this report as a single entity, it is not homogeneous. There are at least two important variables here: types of workers and civil service versus contract workers. With respect to the types of workers, there are differences in disciplines, levels of education, function, lead time for training, availability of workers, economic considerations, and many other dimensions. Additionally, different departments and agencies of the federal government use contract employees to fill a variety of needs. For example, the Department of Energy (DOE) has contracted out many of its national laboratories (they are Government Owned, Contractor Operated [GOCO] facilities); NASA has contracted out much of its engineering and support functions (NASA still manages these facilities, but most of the employees are contractors); the Department of Defense (DoD) has contract employees working as staff employees in the Pentagon, often indistinguishable in function from civil service employees in the same office;

---

[1] For a useful discussion of the problems inherent in measuring the federal workforce in general, see Light, 1999.

[2] As we discuss later, there are no good statistics on the size or composition of the contract workforce, so an exact quantification is not possible for this report. However, it is clear from recent outsourcing of federal jobs in general, and the scale of government acquisitions, that this component of the workforce is very large indeed.

and many departments and agencies have contracted out much of their IT support. In addition to these categories of STEM workers, a large number of contractors build or deliver many products and services that the government needs.

This brief overview suggests that policies for managing the federal STEM workforce require high-quality data.[3] An example of the limitation of STEM generalities is the often-heard assertion that the federal STEM workforce is in crisis, a relatively meaningless statement, in that some portions of the workforce are definitely healthy while others are in need of help, as was illustrated in Chapter Two.

The federal government also needs to take into account the balance between the civil service and contractor workforces. Understanding the factors influencing this balance and the resulting effects at different levels would provide policymakers with a clearer idea of how the nation depends on each component of the STEM workforce, and would permit them more-efficient allocation of resources to meet true national needs. Unfortunately, this balance is currently impossible to determine due to insufficient data for the civil service workforce, and an almost total lack of data for the contractor workforce.[4]

Although no agency keeps centralized, detailed records on the size and composition of its contract workforce, this workforce is large and vitally important to the functions of the federal government. Of the agencies we interviewed, NASA appeared to have the best understanding of its dependence on contract support for the agency as a whole, and so provides an instructive example of this dependence. NASA estimates that two-thirds of its STEM workforce is contracted out, and 71 percent of its contracts support technical research and

---

[3] We will not try to highlight in this report all the elements that will need to be considered, but rather just the types of data that are needed and the issues that STEM leaders should consider.

[4] Note as well that the balance referred to here is not a centrally managed aspect of the federal STEM workforce but rather is the manifestation of policies developed and executed at the various departments and agencies of the federal government on what products to buy and services to outsource.

development (R&D) efforts.[5] Other examples include the DOE STEM workforce located at the national labs, many of which are managed and staffed by contractors, and the significant portion of the DoD STEM workforce employed by the defense contractors that build weapons systems.

Data Requirements for Workforce Analysis and Policy Development

As a prelude to gathering information from federal agencies, we first sought to identify what data and tools would be needed to answer questions about the adequacy of the federal STEM workforce and to develop workforce policies.[6] In general, a principal goal of analyses supporting STEM workforce policies is to develop reliable forecasts of future needs that inform government policymakers as they consider how to address these needs. These policies include such things as recruiting and retention benefits and increased pay or educational opportunities. To understand these requirements, a quick overview of some policy considerations is also in order.

Federal policies on the STEM workforce can be categorized into two important and overlapping domains. The first domain is the adequacy of the national STEM workforce—namely, the pool of STEM talent from which the civil service as well as the private sector (which provides not only the non-federal workforce but also the contractor component of the federal workforce) must draw. This component can be viewed as the STEM *macro-workforce* piece, in that it addresses the environment in which the federal STEM workforce competes for workers (see Chapter Two). At its broadest level, the

---

[5] Contrary to our definition of the federal STEM workforce, these statistics do not include those who work for private-sector companies that build, for example, major end items for NASA. So, for example, the Boeing aerospace workforce working on spacecraft is not included in this number.

[6] With respect to policy development, we do not try to give a comprehensive outline of all factors that need to be considered, but rather those that have direct implications for the types of data that should be collected.

macro-workforce is a global as well as national workforce.[7] The second domain is the adequacy of the civil service STEM workforce and policies to enhance it (e.g., salary and benefit issues, retention incentives). This includes not just the size of the civil service workforce, but also the competitiveness of the workforce in the national and worldwide market for top-notch STEM workers. It should be noted, however, that there is a significant overlap between these two domains caused by the increased flexibility given to government STEM managers to contract out many functions, most notably under OMB Circular A-76, *Performance of Commercial Activities*.[8]

A temporal perspective on STEM workforce goals, policy development, and program effects is also useful. Government policies that affect the national STEM workforce range from the very long term (e.g., policies to influence K–12 STEM education so that the number of students selecting STEM majors as undergraduate and graduate students will be sufficient to meet the needs of the nation), to the medium term (e.g., providing funds for research and student support at U.S. universities), to the relatively short term (e.g., conducting outreach to the private sector to make specific STEM workforce needs known). In almost all cases, developing policy for any of these timeframes requires not only knowledge of the current status of the workforce (both civil service and contractor), but some ability to forecast workforce requirements and status in the future. This ability, in turn, requires the collection and maintenance of current and historical data on the STEM workforce, economic factors, and demographic trends, and other data components necessary for the development of sophisticated models. It is important to note that we are not claiming the ability or the need to predict the future with perfect

---

[7] For example, the development of military hardware frequently involves components built overseas. These workers, though not part of the national U.S. STEM workforce in one sense, can in another sense be viewed as part of the federal STEM workforce in that they produce products for the federal government.

[8] OMB Circular A-76, *Performance of Commercial Activities*, can be found at http://www.whitehouse.gov/omb/circulars/a076/a76_rev2003.pdf.

clarity. Rather, we are saying that decent forecasts, updated periodically, are needed for planning purposes.

The development of macro-workforce policies must be based on an understanding of the supply and demand for STEM workers—a seemingly classical economic problem. Normal economic measures would therefore seem to be useful indicators of the health of the national STEM workforce. Butz et al. (2003) argue that these classical economic indicators (e.g., salary levels, unemployment rate) are reliable gauges for the health of the STEM workforce. Yet, there are several complicating factors, such as the value of filling STEM jobs with U.S. citizens, and the need for an increased number of STEM workers holding security clearances.[9]

If policies for the national STEM workforce can be viewed as addressing macro-workforce issues, policies for the civil service STEM workforce can be viewed as addressing *micro-workforce* issues in that they deal primarily with how the federal government recruits, manages, and retains the talent it needs to serve the nation, rather than policies meant to change the STEM workforce environment in which they recruit and retain. Not surprisingly, the focus of this component is almost entirely on the civil service workforce. Interviews conducted to support this research indicate that by contracting out certain parts of the federal STEM workforce, federal decision makers are not only trying to ensure that top talent will be available to work on critical STEM projects but are outsourcing the STEM recruiting, management, and retention problems to the private sector as well. In the

---

[9] The visibility of the need for STEM workers with security clearances has increased dramatically, and new requirements for STEM workers with clearances have certainly been created since September 11, 2001, but the RAND research team is not aware of any significant increase in the number or percentage of the federal STEM workforce with this requirement. The creation of the Department of Homeland Security (DHS) in and of itself would not have significantly changed this requirement, as it was largely created from existing agencies. There is, however, a requirement that all DHS employees hold a secret security clearance. Furthermore, increases in the size of the Federal Bureau of Investigation (FBI) and some other agencies will have created some additional requirements, but probably not significant ones given the size of the federal STEM workforce of more than 250,000. As with so many other aspects of managing the STEM workforce, this is an area in which there is simply inadequate data to draw conclusions.

view of some senior managers interviewed for this study, the ability to outsource these functions is part of the reason they are willing to pay private-sector firms to supply the needed workers.[10]

The data required to conduct adequate analysis on the macro-workforce issues seem to target those factors that motivate individuals (and perhaps society in general) to value and undertake careers in STEM areas. These factors include such diverse and difficult-to-quantify variables as the quality of K–12 STEM teachers, the structure of degree-producing programs at universities, economic factors that encourage or discourage careers in STEM areas, and many other factors.

The data required for the micro-workforce policy analysis and development are more concrete. Given the macro-workforce forecasts (which provide information on the expected number and quality of workers in the future STEM workforce from which the federal government must recruit, as well as the framework in which the second set of policies must be crafted to succeed), detailed data (historical and current) are needed on standard human resources factors (e.g., pay, benefits, age and education level of the workforce, retirement age). These data would then enable population models to forecast STEM micro-workforce conditions. These forecasts should then be compared with future requirements, which are based on a department or agency's mid-term to long-term staffing plans. These staffing plans are a fundamentally important component of the needed data and one not currently captured, in that it is impossible to make accurate statements on the adequacy of the future STEM workforce without first understanding the future need for workers. In environments in which STEM specialties and needs are quickly evolving, using static requirements instead of forecasts is in many cases not likely to produce a reasonable understanding of future STEM workforce needs.

More succinctly, the data needed to craft competent federal STEM workforce policies include well-supported forecasts of the future national STEM workforce (macro-workforce) environment and

---

[10] Interview by Terrence Kelly and David Adamson with DHS representatives, May 2003.

the requirements for and status of the existing and forecasted federal STEM workforce (primarily civil service workers). Specifically, it is necessary to know such statistics as:

- STEM workforce requirements (historical, current, and forecasted), to include worker demographics (qualification level,[11] age, average age at retirement, etc.)
- Status of STEM workers in STEM jobs (historical, current, and forecasted), to include worker demographics (qualification level, age, eligibility for retirement, etc.)
- Number of STEM workers not in STEM jobs (historical, current, and forecasted)
- The availability of STEM workers (from the macro-workforce current status and forecasts).

Current Data Are Adequate for Some Kinds of Analysis, but Forecasts Are Insufficient

Overall, the data kept by the Office of Personnel Management (OPM) and individual federal departments and agencies, and the data collected by the National Science Foundation (NSF), are not adequate to answer some of the most important questions related to developing comprehensive policies for the federal STEM workforce.[12] Additionally, each department and agency defines and handles the issues of its STEM workforce within the general parameters set out by regulation and OPM guidance, but with its own individual definitions and procedures. For example, OPM has a list of occupation codes that defines the STEM workforce, but NASA does not consider this list specific enough for its own purposes, and so has modified it.

---

[11] Here, we use "qualification level" to include such items as formal education or other qualifications that reflect on a worker's ability to perform, advance, and stay in his or her current STEM field.

[12] We discuss the implications of this lack of data later in this chapter.

Existing data and forecasts (such as those at OPM, NSF, and the Department of Labor [DOL] Bureau of Labor Statistics [BLS]) are sufficient to reach some conclusions about the national STEM workforce—that is, on its size and general qualifications. However, data on federal STEM workforce requirement projections are inadequate.

The federal STEM workforce consists of both civil service and contract employees. However, because the government keeps almost no data on the contract workforce, this discussion will focus primarily on the civil service component. Furthermore, our interviews with the federal departments and agencies indicate that the federal government does not systematically keep forecasts of future STEM workforce requirements. This limits the degree of confidence in forecasts of workforce adequacy, particularly in quickly changing fields such as information technology (IT). The BLS was the only organization that maintained workforce forecasts further out than one year,[13] although NASA is currently conducting an analysis of its civil service needs through an "Employee Preference Survey" that may shed some light on its future needs,[14] and the Centers for Disease Control and Prevention (CDC) and the Agency for Toxic Substances and Disease Registry (ATSDR) also prepare forecasts, but only for one year into the future.[15]

Interviews conducted to support this research indicate that no federal department or agency makes adequate forecasts of future requirements, and this lack of data implies that the BLS predictions

---

[13] However, because labor markets adjust to changing conditions, these projections are often unreliable, though BLS continues to study ways of improving them. For details, see http://data.bls.gov/servlet/oep.nioem.servlet.ActionServlet?Action=empior&MultipleSelect=XXXXXX&Sort=ws_emp_b&StartItem=0&Resort=No&ResortButton=No&Base=2000&Proj=2010&SingleSelect=909100&Type=Industry&Number=All for the BLS projections, and see http://www.bls.gov/emp/nioem/empioan.htm for information on BLS's projection methodology.

[14] Interview by Donna Fossum with NASA representatives, May 2003.

[15] Answers prepared in response to RAND interview questions, May and June 2003. This list of questions constituted the standard template used by RAND in its interviews with all agency representatives.

must be based on the current federal workforce requirements or the application of public-sector trend information to the federal government. Furthermore, in some cases, the BLS forecasts appear to be based not on trends for the actual workforce, but rather on the application of general statistical trends to the existent workforce (i.e., a large number of the STEM specialties in the DOL data base have a forecasted 5-percent loss between 2001 and 2010, indicating that this 5-percent figure is a statistic applied to the current workforce rather than derived from the demographics of it). In general, NSF, OPM, and BLS data, and separate analysis done by the Department of Commerce (DOC), indicate the following:

- Notwithstanding what the numbers show, during interviews conducted for this study, more than one agency cited the availability of quality STEM workers as their biggest concern. In particular, NASA representatives stated that the agency's biggest concern in the long term is the dwindling pipeline of STEM workers,[16] and Department of Transportation (DOT) representatives cited the declining numbers of engineers graduating with the specific skill sets needed by the department and the difficulty in keeping up with the changing technical skills required by the transportation industry as their largest concerns.[17]
- There do not appear to be widely collected data on the quality of civil service STEM workers (e.g., universities from which they graduated, publication history, or even years of experience).

Issues Facing Managers of the Federal STEM Workforce

As previously noted, the federal STEM workforce consists of both civil service and contract employees, and the government keeps almost no data on the contract workforce, limiting this discussion pri-

---

[16] Interview by Donna Fossum and Gabrielle Bloom with NASA representatives, May 2003.

[17] Interview by David Adamson with DOT representatives, June 2003.

marily to the civil service STEM workforce. Nonetheless, our observations indicate a need for policies and programs to make civil service STEM opportunities more attractive, and these issues play a central role in what we have termed the *micro-workforce policy domain.* Our observations into the real situation faced by the federal government call into question some of the alarmist assertions sounded about the pending crisis in the civil service STEM workforce. Nevertheless, the impressions of many federal government STEM personnel managers also make it clear that there may be real issues requiring attention.

The Federal STEM Workforce Is Aging

The civil service STEM workforce is aging (see Figure 3.1). The surge in requirements for STEM workers in the post-Sputnik era created a bulge in the STEM population, which now is reaching retirement age.[18] There is a need to replenish this workforce with workers possessing appropriate skills and experience, as indicated by the following findings:

- DoD retirement data show that the percentage of the DoD's STEM workforce eligible to retire will more than double, from 29.1 percent in June 2002 to 69.5 percent in June 2012, according to a Defense Management Data Center (DMDC) briefing (Eitelberg and Lauter, 2002).
- Both NASA and NIH anticipate similar increases.[19]
- In an interview we conducted with NASA representatives,[20] they stated that impending retirements of its aging STEM workforce (25 percent of whom are eligible to retire in the next five years [through 2008]) is one of its major short-term to medium-term concerns.

---

[18] A similar bulge may exist in the IT workforce based on the tremendous increases in requirements for IT specialties over the past two decades.

[19] For NASA projections, see the *NASA Workforce* Web site at http://nasapeople.nasa.gov/workforce/data/page4.htm. For NIH projections, see National Institutes of Health, 2001.

[20] Interview by Donna Fossum and Gabrielle Bloom with NASA representatives, May 2003.

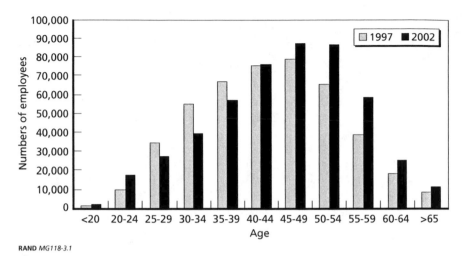

RAND *MG118-3.1*

SOURCE: OPM *FedScope* database.

FIGURE 3.1—Age of Federal Employees in STEM Occupations

Despite the concerns of various departments and agencies, a May 2003 article in *Government Executive* (Friel, 2003) makes the point that retirement eligibility and actual retirements are two different things. The article states that "federal employees rarely opt for early retirement" and that "federal workers generally wait four to six years after becoming eligible [for retirement] before retiring. In 2001, the U.S. General Accounting Office (GAO) estimated that 37 percent of workers who became eligible to retire by 2006 would wait more than a decade to leave."

Indicators suggest that a significant percentage of STEM workers who leave federal employment head for the private-sector workforce, although this tendency is not uniform across specialties, level of education, or age groups. However, the turnover rate in the federal workforce in general is actually quite low. In fact, according to the *Government Executive* article, "no other industry can claim a lower turnover rate than the federal government." Specific evidence to this effect includes the following:

- A DMDC study indicates that of the Research, Development, Test, and Evaluation (RDT&E) STEM employees who left federal service between June 2000 and December 2001, 56 percent left for "greener pastures" (defined as leaving to join private-sector firms, for promotion opportunities or higher salaries, or to pursue career goals or opportunities). Leaving for greener pastures accounted for 58.5 percent of male departures and 47.4 percent of female departures.[21] However, these departures represent less than 2 percent of the DoD STEM workforce.[22]

- The same DMDC study indicates that for RDT&E STEM employees, almost half of those who left for "greener pastures" were in their 30s. Furthermore, the study showed that the propensity to leave increased with education level. As a percentage of those who left for "greener pastures" at each degree level, 50.2 percent were bachelor's degree holders, 66.8 percent were master's degree holders, and 72.2 percent were Ph.D. holders.

- NASA foresees similar problems, with approximately 25 percent of all NASA employees eligible to retire in the next five years and the smallest age group of NASA employees being under the age of 30 (e.g., NASA has 1,163 employees over the age of 60, and only 443 under 30, as of May 2003).[23]

- NIH seems to face a similar problem with impending retirements, with almost 70 percent of its population of senior investigators (the largest and a critical component of its doctoral population) having received their doctorates prior to 1980 and 26 percent prior to 1970.

- There are indications that scientists tend to stay on for a longer period past retirement age than most other workers, thus lessening concerns over the effect of retirements on the workforce.

---

[21] Defense Management Data Center, 2002. This data is further broken down by age and education level in the DMDC briefing.

[22] DoD STEM retention was better than for the general DoD civil service population. A total of 1,531 left during the 18-month period out of approximately 85,000 in the DoD STEM workforce.

[23] Interview by Donna Fossum and Gabrielle Bloom with NASA representatives, May 2003.

As stated in Friel (2003), "Agriculture's scientists tend to stay more than four years past retirement age, while clerical workers tend to retire within a year or two. That turns out to be true at other agencies, such as NASA and the National Institutes of Health."[24]

The "aging of the workforce," as indicated by the disproportionate number of older workers as compared with younger workers, overlooks the recruiting patterns of the federal government. For the general civil service workforce, 70 percent of government hires in 2002 were over the age of 30.[25] There does seem to be a slight aging trend in the STEM workforce. However, a careful look at Figure 3.1 also indicates a substantial number of older STEM workers were hired by the federal government during the time period (1997–2002) in question. (Note, for example, that the total number of workers in the 45–49 age group in 2002 is significantly larger than the total number in the 40–44 age group in 1997.) But, the 45–49 age group in 2002 is simply the 40–44 age group five years later, indicating that many workers were hired into this group between 1997 and 2002. In other words, the aging of the federal STEM workforce is due at least in part to hiring decisions, not just the inevitable progress of time and tenure.

Workforce Incentives Are Effective but Not Widely Used
Workforce incentives seem to be a good way to attract and retain quality, higher-end STEM workers, as are innovative efforts to make professional life in government agencies more appealing, although this research effort did not identify any comprehensive analysis of incentive effectiveness for federal government employee recruitment or retention. Many of these programs designed to make government-agency employment more appealing exist only in agencies with very special missions requiring exceptional talent, such as NASA and

---

[24] Friel, May 2003, p.26.

[25] Friel, May 2003, p. 30.

CDC. However, this statement is based on anecdotal evidence, as we were unable to find comprehensive data on the issue. Nevertheless, that anecdotal evidence suggests the following:

- Some agencies have had or anticipate success with aggressive recruiting and retention techniques. For example, the CDC and ATSDR prepare a recruiting plan that addresses the gains, losses, predicted retirements, and racial breakdown of their workforces and are placing more emphasis on using noncompetitive authorities in the recruiting process, including the Persons with Disabilities Program, Veteran Readjustment Program, Outstanding Scholar, Bilingual/Bicultural Program, Presidential Management Intern (PMI) Program, Student Career Experience Program, Hispanic Association of Colleges and Universities (HACU) National Internship Program, other student programs, and the various hiring flexibilities offered under Title 42 of the U.S. Code. The CDC also uses other recruiting tools, such as recruitment and relocation bonuses, and above-the-minimum starting salaries when justified.
- The CDC has also developed and implemented several fellowship and training programs for scientists and health professionals under several statutory authorities.[26] Each program is designed

[26] Examples of these programs include the Epidemic Intelligence Service (EIS), a postgraduate training program for medical officers and other health professionals interested in the practice of epidemiology. This program was initiated in 1951 and provides valuable training mainly to Commissioned Corps and Service Fellow participants in one of the predominant public health occupations at CDC. Typically, about 70 individuals are selected each year to participate in the program. EIS officers conduct front-line national and international epidemiologic activities, including disease investigations, public health surveillance, and dissemination of public health information. Graduates of the training are considered highly qualified in the field of epidemiology, and approximately 60 percent are ultimately employed on a permanent basis at CDC, either in the Commissioned Corps or civil service. The CDC has also established a fellowship program for scientists to promote research and studies. Approximately 330 Service Fellows are currently employed on temporary excepted service appointments to accomplish special projects and initiatives. Because the benefit package is similar to that of the civil service, and the appointment may be extended, many Fellows do not find it necessary to compete for permanent positions. The CDC conducted a number of statistical analyses to determine to what extent this resource pool has contributed to its permanent workforce. Over a four-year period (January 1996 to March 2000), 39.5

to provide targeted work experiences and/or training for partici-pants in occupational specialties that are necessary to accom-plishing the CDC's mission of protecting the nation's health and building its public health systems. As such, program gradu-ates may be considered to be part of the labor pool when the CDC recruits for permanent workforce positions and seeks can-didates for positions in the public health system at the national, state, and local levels.[27]

- A recent CDC-specific training statutory authority has enabled the CDC to develop and implement targeted training programs. A good example of these programs is the Public Health Preven-tion Service (PHPS), initiated in 1997 and enhanced in July 2000, to provide master's-degree-level public health profession-als with training and rotational work assignments at the CDC and at state and local health departments. The program is de-signed to train about 25 health professionals per year, who are then employed in the local, state, and federal public health workforce.[28]

- The CDC reports success with retention bonuses of up to 25 percent of a scientist's base pay. Additionally, in-service training for employees seems to be successful at maintaining a well-trained workforce.[29]

- NASA, too, has aggressive recruiting schemes in place. It has re-newed its emphasis on advertising for and recruitment of STEM personnel. The Agency developed the National Recruitment Ini-

---

percent of eligible Fellows made the transition to a permanent position with the agency. This finding clearly underscores the critical importance of the fellowship program as a recruitment source for CDC's permanent STEM workforce.

[27] Response from CDC representative to RAND's interview questionnaire.

[28] Response to RAND's interview questionnaire. Graduates from this program are very competitive when seeking employment. From the first PHPS graduating class in 2000, nine graduates were hired by the CDC, and the balance of the class was hired by key public health partner organizations, such as state health departments.

[29] Response by Department of Health and Human Services (DHHS) officials to RAND questionnaire, subsequent to telephone interviews conducted by Mihal Gross with DHHS official on June 6, 2003.

tiative to identify new techniques available for recruiting STEM personnel and to explain those techniques to its internal human resources staff.[30]

- NASA has had success attracting and retaining a top-notch scientific workforce by using authority granted by the OPM to offer salaries above the civil service rate and by using NASA's "Schedule A" hiring authority.[31] NASA representatives told us, however, that retaining scientists and retaining engineers are two separate challenges. Scientists tend to stay at NASA because of the fresh scientific challenges that NASA provides and the unique work it offers. NASA's engineering workforce, however, tends to be more market-sensitive and therefore more difficult to retain.[32] Furthermore, two agencies (the Department of Homeland Security [DHS] and DOT) cited NASA's ability to pay higher salaries and offer special incentives as two capabilities that they felt would help them to manage their STEM workforces, should they be given such authority by the OPM.[33]

Citizenship Issues Do Not Appear to Pose a Major Problem

Citizenship requirements for federal STEM employees have taken on additional importance since September 11, 2001. The new Department of Homeland Security, for example, requires that all DHS employees hold at least an interim secret-level clearance. However, many of these employees work for agencies (e.g., the U.S. Border Patrol, Customs, and the Coast Guard) that transferred to the DHS upon its activation and that would already have required many employees to have these clearances. Furthermore, the CDC's Title 5 employees are all U.S. citizens. However, despite this seemingly large requirement for secret-level security clearances, there does not seem to be a re-

---

[30] Interview by Donna Fossum and Gabrielle Bloom with NASA representatives, May 2003.

[31] Schedule A employees are non-permanent, and the agency has more flexibility in hiring and managing them.

[32] Interview by Donna Fossum and Gabrielle Bloom with NASA representatives, May 2003.

[33] Terrence Kelly and David Adamson interview with Assistant Secretary Penrose Albright, May 2003, and David Adamson interview with DOT representatives, June 2003.

quirement for a larger number of STEM workers who are U.S. citizens, when the entire federal STEM workforce of more than a quarter of a million workers is taken into account.[34]

Implications

Given the limited data that are available, and the anecdotal evidence presented in this chapter, we can conclude that the federal STEM workforce should be closely monitored to assure its adequacy and stability. In Chapter Five, we present the elements of a data collection plan that will help U.S. STEM personnel managers to monitor the federal STEM workforce and develop policies as needed. In the next chapter, we discuss the policy mechanisms that have been in place and present information about their effectiveness.

---

[34] According to the OPM, there were 276,851 federal STEM workers as of December 31, 2002.

CHAPTER FOUR

Mechanisms for Influencing the Size and Composition of the STEM Workforce

This chapter examines the mechanisms for influencing the size and composition of the STEM workforce, focusing on the federal mechanisms that have been used to do so historically. These mechanisms have been implemented both legislatively by Congress and programmatically by individual federal agencies.

The chapter addresses three questions:

- What are the main mechanisms the federal government has used to shape both its own and the nation's STEM workforce more broadly?
- What are some examples of legislation and programs that have used these various mechanisms?
- What, if any, evidence exists regarding the relative effectiveness of particular mechanisms?

For data on legislation and programs, we drew from archival sources on federal legislative histories (*Congressional Universe* and *Thomas*),[1] the 2002 *Catalog of Federal Domestic Assistance* (CFDA),[2]

---

[1] *The Congressional Universe* is a Lexis-Nexus database that can be found at http://web.lexis-nexis.com/congcomp/. *Thomas* is a Library of Congress Web site. It can be found at http://thomas.loc.gov/.

[2] See General Services Administration, 2002.

and agency-specific sources, as well as a brief survey of the literature on U.S. STEM workforce issues and STEM education.[3]

Historical Overview

Prior to World War II, federal STEM workforce efforts were sporadic and small-scale. They focused initially on building institutions for training STEM professionals, most notably engineers. The earliest federal initiative to shape the STEM workforce was the founding of West Point, the nation's first military academy, whose initial purpose was training Army engineers. During the 19th century, militarily trained engineers exerted a major influence on many arenas of civil engineering, such as railroad and bridge design (O'Connell, 1985, p. 88).

A more broad-based intervention was the Morrill Act of 1862. Although primarily aimed at improving agricultural practice and work skills, this Act also spurred the development of science and engineering programs in every state. Specifically, under the provisions of the Morrill Act, the federal government actually gave states land, and in return states were free to use the land to build facilities on it or sell it and use the proceeds to create institutions for agricultural and technological training. Some states combined these facilities into a single institution, such as Purdue University and Ohio State. Other states created separate technical institutions, such as Virginia Polytechnic Institute. The Morrill Act spurred a transformation in U.S. higher education, one result of which was creation of the U.S. research university system between the 1860s and the early 20th century (Rudolph, 1962, pp. 264–286).

In later years, particularly after World War II when the institutional framework for U.S. STEM training and employment was largely in place via the research university system, the federal role focused on funding and strengthening STEM education and employing

---

[3] Useful overviews of the U.S. STEM workforce debate can be found in Goldman and Massy, 1999, and Jackson, 2002.

STEM services on a massive scale, primarily for R&D. This linkage was cemented by the creation of the National Science Foundation in 1950 and the meteoric increase in agency R&D spending during the Cold War, much of which included some education and training component, often in the form of graduate research assistantships.

A watershed event in federal participation in strengthening the nation's STEM workforce was the passage of the National Defense Education Act of 1958. The NDEA inaugurated large-scale federal funding of K–12 education, especially curricular reform and teacher training in math and science. The act also made federal funds widely available for loans to undergraduates, fellowships for science graduate students, and K–12 science and math curriculum-development projects headed by university scientists.

The NDEA set a precedent for federal involvement in U.S. education, including assistance for STEM education at all levels. This involvement has been increasing ever since. For example, the Elementary and Secondary Education Act and Higher Education Act of 1965 codified the broad dimensions of the current federal role in education, which involves general assistance to states, districts, and institutions, as well as a broad range of assistance for special programs and projects, including many in STEM areas. In addition, three federal agencies—NSF, NASA, and NIH—have specific STEM education missions and provide substantial funds for pre-college programs as well as for undergraduate, graduate, and postdoctoral studies in STEM fields. Today, support from the federal government for STEM programs emphasizes graduate education. Indeed, approximately 20 percent of all full-time STEM graduate students in 1999 cited the federal government as their primary source of support. Because this figure does not include student loans guaranteed by the federal government, the percentage of those who receive some support from the federal government is undoubtedly much higher.[4]

---

[4] See National Science Board, 2002b, Appendix Table 2-27 (available at http://www.nsf.gov/sbe/srs/seind02/pdf/at02.pdf).

Overview of Federal Efforts to Shape the STEM Workforce

What instruments has the federal government used to play a pivotal role in building the STEM workforce? Examining the mechanisms used by the federal government to influence the U.S. and federal STEM workforces, we found that they fall into two broad groups: (1) influencing the STEM pipeline and (2) shaping and developing the current federal STEM workforce. The first group focuses on education and training designed to enhance interest in STEM careers or to support students pursuing STEM degrees. Related to these pipeline-filling measures are immigration policies that affect the size of the U.S. STEM labor pool by relaxing or tightening restrictions on immigrants with STEM skills (e.g., H-1B visa applicants).

The second group of mechanisms focuses on federal initiatives to recruit and retain STEM professionals within the government workforce. These initiatives have typically targeted specific STEM fields or particular demographic groups (such as ethnic minorities or women) or served to recruit students into a particular agency's STEM workforce. There have also been related initiatives that affect STEM workers but which are not specifically targeted toward them. We discuss examples of all of these mechanisms in more detail later in the chapter. In general, the federal government has made far more extensive use of the pipeline-filling mechanisms than of the workforce-shaping mechanisms. It is worth noting that the two mechanisms overlap—influencing the pipeline ultimately shapes the workforce. Their ultimate goals are similar, but they exert their influences at different periods of time. Mechanisms that influence the pipeline exert influence in education, whereas mechanisms for shaping the workforce affect employees.

We found no comprehensive federal initiative focused specifically and exclusively on the federal STEM workforce as an entity.[5] Instead, legislation targeting the U.S. STEM workforce has empha-

---

[5] Thomas (http://loc.thomas.gov) and Congressional Universe (http://web.lexis-nexis.com/congcomp/).

sized certain aspects of the pipeline. As noted in Chapter Three, the federal STEM workforce itself is not homogeneous—it varies considerably from agency to agency. The history of federal initiatives mirrors this pattern—that is, nearly all of the relevant workforce initiatives have been agency-specific initiatives or interagency efforts involving R&D agencies with a particular interest in scientific activities. NIH, for example, offers student-loan repayment programs for researchers who serve a specified term of service in health research. CDC has similar programs.

We found only one example of a federally focused workforce initiative that crossed agencies. Specifically, the Federal Cyber Service Scholarship for Service Program[6] funded by NSF created new university programs to train information assurance professionals. This program also pays education expenses for a limited number of students in return for two years of service with a federal agency. As we discuss later, there has been a good deal of enthusiasm for this type of program, but implementation has been plagued by difficulties with interagency coordination and agency jurisdictional issues.

The legislative underpinnings for federal programs vary by agency. Three agencies with specific science education missions— NSF, NIH, and NASA—trace their authority for such activities back to their initial authorizing legislation. For example, NSF traces its authority to the 1950 *National Science Foundation Authorization Act,* and NIH traces its authority to the 1944 *Public Health Service Act.* Many other STEM educational initiatives cite as their enabling legislation either the 1965 *Elementary and Secondary Education Act* (ESEA), which was re-authorized in 2001 as the *No Child Left Behind Act,* or the 1965 *Higher Education Act,* both of which remain defining pieces of legislation for federal involvement in U.S. education.

Other agencies that lack specific STEM education missions trace their legislative authority to other sources. In some instances, that authority may come from special legislation. So, for example, the 1990 National Environmental Education Act authorized the Envi-

---

[6] See http://www.ehr.nsf.gov/ehr/due/programs/sfs/ for more information.

ronmental Protection Agency (EPA) to create programs to train K–12 instructors in environmental issues and environmental sciences. Alternatively, the authority may be embodied in provisions included in the agency's authorization legislation for a particular year. So, for example, the National Highway Institute in the Department of Transportation awards engineering training and education fellowships to states under the Eisenhower Fellowship program, for which state employees and university students are eligible. This program traces its origins to the Transportation Equity Act of 1998, which was the federal highway and mass-transit authorization bill for that particular year.

The number of mechanisms used in federal initiatives to influence the size and composition of the STEM workforce is relatively small. Here we attempt to categorize and define these mechanisms in more detail. The overview that follows is not intended to be an exhaustive catalog of all federal programs in these areas, but rather a set of illustrative examples of the various mechanisms. For the most part, these mechanisms are not pieces of distinct legislation, but programs embedded in legislation or authorized by agency missions. As discussed earlier, there are two areas that have been targeted: (1) influencing the STEM pipeline and (2) shaping the current federal STEM workforce.

We have divided these mechanisms into the following five categories. The first three are pipeline-influencing mechanisms, and the other two are directed toward shaping the STEM workforce.

- **General interest building:** This category involves heightening enthusiasm for science and potential interest in science fields and careers among K–12 students. This category has also included public education campaigns conducted through the media to improve the image of science as a stimulating and rewarding career.
- **Steering and guidance:** This mechanism includes guidance counseling and apprenticeships that help to place recent or soon-to-be high school graduates into college programs or STEM careers.

- **Resources for higher education:** This mechanism includes funding for undergraduate, graduate, and postgraduate education for scientific fields in the form of grants, loans, or loan guarantees for individual students; tuition assistance; and scholarships and fellowships.
- **Adjusting the labor pool:** This mechanism involves immigration quotas to enlarge or shrink the numbers of STEM workers allowed to enter the U.S. on work (H-1B) visas.
- **Workforce management and development:** Mechanisms in this category include incentives for recruiting and retaining STEM professionals (e.g., providing higher pay, hiring bonuses, or loan forgiveness or repayment) to attract workers to particular STEM fields or occupations, improve STEM skills, retain STEM workers, or influence separation or retirement decisions.

General Interest Building

Typically, interest-building activities have targeted K–12 students, and occasionally the general public, to encourage students' entry into STEM fields of study. We include in this category K–12 teacher training initiatives and incentives, as well as efforts to improve the K–12 science curriculum.

Programs in this category are intended to increase interest among K–12 students in STEM fields and careers. Historically, the federal government's main role in this area has been to fund programs, rather than to design or implement them. More recently (under, for example, the No Child Left Behind Act of 2001), the federal government has also mandated broad standards for assessing the effectiveness of such programs.

Teacher Training

The federal role in funding and promoting STEM teacher training dates back to the early 1950s when the newly created National Science Foundation began its modestly funded summer institutes and workshops for K–12 science teachers. The NDEA in 1958 substantially increased funding for these activities, which the Elementary and Secondary Education Act of 1965 increased further.

The National Science Foundation supports a range of programs in this area, such as Centers for Learning and Teaching, which focus on recruiting, training, and retaining math and science teachers. NASA also has traditionally been heavily involved in these activities. NASA's teacher and faculty preparation programs are designed to involve educators in NASA-related activities through workshops and laboratory and experimental experiences. Almost 400,000 educators participated in NASA programs in fiscal year (FY) 2000, 67 percent of whom were K–12 teachers (Jesse, 2002). An EPA program primarily but not exclusively about STEM education is the Environmental Education and Training Program. Currently led by the University of Wisconsin, Stevens Point, the program trains educational professionals to understand and teach environmental awareness and environmental science (authorized under the National Environmental Education Act).

Curriculum Development
This mechanism is intended to enhance the quality of science and math education by improving educational and training materials. Since the passage of the NDEA in 1958, the federal science establishment has paid considerable attention to strengthening the K–12 science and math curriculum.

Some current federal programs in this area include:

- Instructional Materials Development (sponsored by NSF)—a program that emphasizes the development, dissemination, and implementation of instructional materials and assessments for STEM education
- Star Program schools (sponsored by the U.S. Department of Education)—innovative programs to improve math and science education that pair federal resources with funds and program designs from a state or local educational agency

- Curricular materials developed by the National Institutes of Health.[7]

School Outreach

This category of mechanisms includes programs for heightening K–12 student awareness of and interest in science and STEM activities and fields. A notable favorite in this category has been the summer institute, an educational program first launched in the 1950s by the National Science Foundation.

Numerous federal agencies (among them, NASA and the Department of Transportation) have school outreach programs. NASA in particular has a history of extensive outreach and interest-building programs. In FY 2000, more than one million students participated in NASA education activities, most of whom were K–12 students (Jesse, 2002). Other programs recruit and support underrepresented minorities at all education levels. NASA's participation in such programs is authorized by its founding legislation, the National Aeronautics and Space Act of 1958.

As noted earlier, NSF also makes extensive use of such programs. For example, its Informal Science Education Program provides educational experiences for STEM learning outside of formal classroom environments through the media, public exhibits, and community-based programming.

Summer institutes have often been a popular form of school outreach. In recent years, summer institutes have also evolved into more-specialized forms of training aimed at encouraging undergraduates to enter graduate school in STEM fields. For example, NSF and NIH jointly established the Bioengineering and Bioinformatics Summer Institutes Program to increase the number of young people considering careers in bioengineering and bioinformatics (the use of information technology in the life sciences) at the graduate level and beyond (General Services Administration, 2002). "The aim of this program is to provide students majoring in the biological sciences,

---

[7] For more information on NIH curriculum supplements see the NIH Office of Science Education Web site at http://science.education.nih.gov.

computer sciences, engineering, mathematics, and physical sciences with interdisciplinary bioengineering or bioinformatics research and education experiences."[8]

University-School Partnerships

University-school partnerships, typically funded through federal grants, encompass a range of programs that combine aspects of teacher training, curriculum development, and general outreach. These programs support instruction in several ways: by developing curricular materials and resources, by inviting teachers to participate at university labs, and by bringing university students to schools to help directly in classroom instruction (Williams, 2002, p. xii). NSF's Math-Science Partnership programs are one example of this mechanism. In accordance with the No Child Left Behind Act, the Department of Education has created the Mathematics and Science Partnerships Program, which provides authority for matching grants to create similar partnership programs.

A more narrowly focused partnership-style initiative that combines partnering with support for STEM university training is NSF's Graduate Fellows in K–12 Education programs.

Illustrative Legislation

National Defense Education Act (1958). The NDEA provided funds for the National Science Foundation to increase the size and scope of programs designed to build interest in STEM education. Summer institutes were conducted primarily to stimulate students' interest in science, mathematics, and modern foreign languages, but they also provided support to other educational areas and efforts, including technical education, regional studies, geography, English as a second language, counseling and guidance, school libraries and librarians, and educational media centers.

Elementary and Secondary Education Act (1965). The ESEA represented the first large-scale federal intervention in elementary and

---

[8] All references to federal assistance programs in this chapter are taken from the *Catalog of Domestic Federal Assistance*, 2003.

secondary education. With its passage, the federal government abandoned the reluctance to exert federal control over K–12 schooling that had been evident in the NDEA and instituted accountability measures and other requirements for school districts.

No Child Left Behind Act (2001). A reauthorization of the ESEA, this act contains a significant STEM provision: It authorizes the Math-Science Partnerships (MSP) Initiative, housed in NSF, which is funded by federal grants with a requirement for matching funds from states or educational institutions. MSP programs can receive up to $200 million to support partnerships among scientists, mathematicians, engineers, and teachers to promote research-based approaches in the classroom and to improve math and science teacher training.

In addition, the Act authorized two categories of activities to be funded through peer-reviewed grants. The first involves "infrastructure partnerships" between states and higher-education institutions to improve STEM education. "Action partnerships" are the second category of activities and consist of regionally focused initiatives.

Steering and Guidance

Steering and guidance mechanisms are intended to bridge the gap between K–12 education and college. These mechanisms have typically taken the form of counseling or other kinds of advising intended to encourage potential workers to seek STEM jobs, both within the federal government and more broadly across all sectors. The major federal counseling programs today have a vocational rather than a STEM emphasis. Particular U.S. agencies with a significant science mission have their own special apprenticeships and internships.

Guidance Counseling

The NDEA authorized funds for states and institutions to create training programs for guidance counselors who could encourage students to pursue STEM careers. The NDEA also provided educational loans to attract students to these counseling positions. Many current programs, in particular those directed toward underrepresented minorities, include a counseling component. Many federal counseling functions have been subsumed by vocational training programs.

Apprenticeships and Internships

Apprenticeship and internship programs are designed to provide students with an early exposure to college or advanced research. Most STEM-specific programs in this area are spearheaded by the NSF, which sometimes collaborates with other agencies on these programs. For example, NSF and the DOE's Office of Science are collaborating on a program that supports students and faculty with eligible NSF projects who are accepted into one of four DOE initiatives that provide hands-on summer research opportunities in DOE national laboratories. Specifically, the names of these programs are Science Undergraduate Research Internships, Faculty and Student Teams, Community College Institute of Science and Technology, and Pre-Service Teacher Internships.

The majority of federal programs in this area appear to have one of two goals: (1) recruiting members of particular demographic groups into STEM fields (NSF's Minority Scientist Internship Program, for example) or (2) recruiting STEM graduates into government employment (the Department of Commerce's internship program to attract students to its engineering programs, for example).

Illustrative Legislation

As with the general interest-building mechanisms, there are no specific steering and guidance statutes aimed primarily at shaping the federal STEM workforce. An example of more general steering and guidance provisions appear in the NDEA, which provided matching grants to states and districts to train high-school guidance counselors and fund counseling positions. The underlying intent was to steer promising high school students to college, although not necessarily into STEM fields of study.

Resources for Higher Education

Another way the federal government encourages individuals to pursue STEM careers is by providing assistance for higher education. A range of mechanisms exists to accomplish this. Those mechanisms are intended to attract university students to STEM majors, to support STEM graduate students, and to fund postdoctoral positions that help STEM Ph.D.s transition into the professional labor force. Federal support may take the form of formula grants,[9] block grants, or project grants awarded competitively to eligible units of government (states, counties, cities, or school districts), educational institutions, or individuals.

The federal government remains a major source of support for STEM higher education in the United States, particularly at the graduate level, though levels of support vary substantially across fields. For example, as of 1999, federal aid constituted the primary source of support for a high percentage of students in the physical sciences (such as atmospheric science [61 percent] and astronomy [48 percent]). By contrast, federal funds were not a significant avenue of support for graduate students in the social sciences, psychology, or mathematics.

The basic assistance mechanisms include grants; scholarships, fellowships, and assistantships; and loans and work-study programs. Trends in federal higher education funding suggest that loans to individuals and block grants to states are becoming the most frequently used mechanisms. In recent federal budgets, block grant consolidations have moved programs out of the federal government's purview, giving states leeway to design their own programs. For example, appropriations for the Eisenhower Professional Development (EPD) grants—which are administered by several federal agencies—are

---

[9] Formula grants, according to the CFDA, are "allocations of money to States or their subdivisions in accordance with distribution formulas prescribed by law or administrative regulation, for activities of a continuing nature not confined to a specific project" (General Services Administration, 2002).

rolled into state grants for improving teacher quality, contingent on performance evaluations and student test scores (Jesse, 2002).

The student populations targeted by these federal mechanisms vary widely. For example, eligibility for federal assistance may be needs based (as under the Pell Grants program) or merit based (as with many scholarships and fellowships). Funds may also be available to students in particular fields (such as cyber security) or demographic groups (such as women or ethnic minorities).

Grants

Grants are, in effect, a gift from the federal government given for a specific purpose. Grant recipients vary widely—they may be states, local governments, institutions, consortia, or individuals. An early instance of federal grant support for STEM-related training was the Morrill Act of 1862, which gave states 30,000 acres of land per each state's U.S. congressional representative and senator. The land could be used or sold, but the proceeds had to be devoted to creating institutions for improving agricultural, engineering, and vocational training. Currently, the largest federal grant program for higher education is the Pell Grant program for undergraduates, which pays tuition and expenses. Pell grants are needs-based grants that are not STEM-specific. Other examples of grants are the health grant programs for creating health care training centers in medically underserved areas and for training underrepresented minorities in health professions.

Scholarships, Fellowships, and Assistantships

Scholarships, fellowships, and assistantships are typically awarded to individual students and may be either merit based or needs based. NSF has the longest-running scholarship programs, but all of the major federal science agencies (such as NASA, NIH, DOE, Department of Education, and DoD) use some form of these mechanisms:

- Scholarships: These awards are typically given to undergraduate students.
- Fellowships and assistantships (usually graduate, some postdoctoral): These forms of assistance are the most common among

STEM graduate students who rely on federal funding for the majority of their financial support. The use of particular mechanisms varies significantly by field. Students in physical sciences are supported mainly by research assistantships (42 percent of physical sciences graduate students) and tuition assistance (11 percent).

- Research assistantships are also important in engineering (42 percent of engineering graduate students) and earth, atmospheric, and ocean sciences (41 percent of those students). In mathematics, however, primary student support is through teaching assistantships (57 percent of mathematics graduate students) and self-support (17 percent). Students in social sciences were mainly self-supporting (41 percent) or used teaching assistantships (22 percent) (National Science Board, 2002a, Ch. 2).

Loans, Loan Guarantees, and Work-Study

Loans are now the most common form of federal assistance for higher education. Since 1958, when the NDEA was passed, the federal government has made loans available to undergraduates and graduate students. Currently, there is a vast array of federal loan programs. They include direct loans, loan guarantees, and private, unsecured loans (a helpful summary of federal student loan programs appears in Kilburn and Asch, 2003).

Under current law, federally guaranteed loans are not tied to STEM fields or targeted to academic disciplines. Historically, eligibility for these programs had been based primarily on need. Now, there are numerous federal loan programs, some of which are need based and some of which are not. The only federal loan program specifically aimed at STEM students is targeted to health professionals through DHHS. This loan program (authorized by the Public Health Services Act of 1944, augmented by the Health Professions Education Partnerships Act of 1998) is intended to offset the high cost of medical training by providing low-interest loans to qualified students. Funds are allocated according to a formula and are used to capitalize loan funds at specific institutions.

Federal loans may also include funds for facilities and equipment used in specific STEM-related programs. The Federal Aviation Administration (FAA) in the Department of Transportation, for example, operates a program that pays student for the costs incurred in using FAA facilities and equipment.

The trend in federal support for higher education students has seen a gradual shift from grants and scholarships to loans. The practice of borrowing from the federal government has become so widespread that the majority of all students enrolled at U.S. colleges and universities now rely on some form of federal loan.

Illustrative Legislation

Morrill Act (1862). This act represented the first large-scale federal intervention in American higher education. Passed during the Civil War, when the interests in the South that had opposed a prior version of the Act were not present in Congress to contest it, the Morrill Act of 1862 made it possible for the new western states to establish colleges and for many eastern states to open new universities and technical colleges. More than 70 "land grant" colleges were established under the original Morrill Act; a second act in 1890 extended the provisions to the 16 southern states and created separate institutions for blacks in states where segregation barred their access to college. Although originally started as agricultural and technical schools, many of the new institutions grew into large public universities that over the years have educated millions of students who otherwise might not have been able to afford college. States still receive federal grants (determined by population-based formulas) for agricultural research under the provisions of this Act, as renewed and amended.

GI Bill Act (1944). The GI Bill Act did not directly address the STEM workforce. However, it swelled the numbers of U.S. college students, which in turn exerted pressure on policymakers to find ways of improving college preparation and infusing more resources into the educational system. Between 1940 and 1960, attendance at U.S. universities quadrupled (Montgomery, 1994), from less than 2 million to nearly 8 million. The principal reason for this growth in enrollment was the GI Bill, the 1944 legislation that paid college expenses for

World War II veterans who served for more than 90 days in the military after 1940. Benefits were given as grants paid directly to colleges, up to a maximum of $500 a year for tuition, books, fees, and other training costs. This program ended in 1956. In the peak year of 1947, veterans accounted for 49 percent of college enrollment. Out of a veteran population of 15.4 million, some 7.8 million received an education courtesy of the GI Bill.[10]

National Defense Education Act (1958). Loan assistance specifically for STEM students first appears in the NDEA, which offered loans of up to $1,000 per year to a maximum of $5,000 per undergraduate student. Funds for loans were allotted on a state-by-state basis, using population-based formulas. Although preference for these loans was to be given to students in STEM fields, there was no mechanism for enforcing this preference, and so students in a variety of disciplines received support.

Health Professions Education Partnerships Act (1998). This Act, which amended the Public Health Service Act of 1944, created Public Health Training Centers[11] to train health care professionals. These Centers are partnerships between accredited schools of public health and related health and academic institutions and public health agencies and organizations (Health Resources and Services Administration, n.d.).

Adjusting the Labor Pool

The previous three categories of mechanisms are all designed to fill the STEM pipeline. The final two categories focus on managing the current STEM workforce.[12] The workforce literature indicates that there are several general tools for accomplishing this.

---

[10] For more information on the current educational assistance program, known as the Montgomery GI Bill, see http://www.gibill.va.gov/education/GI_Bill.htm.

[11] These centers support graduate-level public health education programs.

[12] Our principal information source for the discussion of these two categories is Levy et al. (2001).

The first mechanism for broadening the labor pool centers on immigration policy. One way in which the federal government can shape the STEM workforce is by altering the pool of qualified STEM talent by "importing" professionals from abroad through more permissive immigration policies. A series of laws have set annual quotas for the number of H-1B visa workers allowed to immigrate to the United States. Current law sets caps on the number of H-1B visas (for scientific and technical workers). This cap has been adjusted up and down in recent years, both in response to perceived workforce needs in the private sector and in response to complaints from labor groups and others that immigrant STEM workers were taking jobs from Americans.

Illustrative Legislation
Immigration Reform Act of 1990, Competitiveness Act of 1998, American Competitiveness in the 21st Century Act of 2000. The 1990 Immigration Reform Act set a ceiling of 65,000 on the number of H-1B visa holders allowed to work in STEM positions in the United States at any given time. The most recent legislation, the Competitiveness Act of 2001, revised the ceiling at 195,000 STEM immigrants per year. There are currently competing proposals in Congress on this issue: One would expand the current cap above 200,000, while the other would cut it back to 65,000 as of 2005. In general, labor and STEM groups back reducing the cap, while business supports raising it.[13]

Workforce Shaping and Development

Besides addressing the supply of STEM workers, federal policy also includes measures directed at developing and maintaining the federal STEM workforce. These include policies and laws developed to recruit and retain a first-class STEM workforce.

---

[13] "U.S. Immigration Reform: Positive or Negative?" 2002.

Recruiting

Recruiting involves bringing new members into the STEM workforce. Recruitment programs typically rely on three mechanisms: (1) hiring bonuses, (2) pay or benefit incentives, or (3) student loan forgiveness/repayment. There are no government-wide programs to recruit STEM workers using these specific mechanisms. Instead, existing programs using these mechanisms are agency-specific.

- **Hiring bonuses.** Our interviews with agencies found that only NASA appears to be using hiring bonuses on a regular basis. Under the Code of Federal Regulations, agencies can receive temporary authority from OPM to offer bonuses for recruiting to meet special needs. Interviews with NASA officials revealed that they have sought and received such authority to meet specific personnel needs in the past. Other agencies also indicated that such authority would benefit their STEM workforce.
- **Loan forgiveness or repayment.** Currently, the National Institutes of Health has a program to repay outstanding student loans for health researchers. The program pays eligible health researchers up to $35,000 per year in loan repayments and $13,000 per year in federal tax credits. To receive these payments, workers must commit to working for NIH for three years. Two of NASA's centers, the Kennedy Space Center and the Johnson Space Center, have similar loan repayment programs. Since the enactment of the NDEA, the federal government has also offered loan forgiveness for a special portion of the STEM workforce: mathematics and science K–12 teachers. Currently, such teachers who work in low-income schools can have up to $5,000 of their federally guaranteed student loans forgiven. This program in its current form is not targeted specifically toward STEM teachers.
- **Scholarships for service.** In this type of program, students receive tuition assistance and a stipend and in return agree to work for a specific period of time in the federal government. The Cyber Service Scholarships program, mentioned earlier, is also a recruiting mechanism. As currently implemented, it is similar to a

loan forgiveness program in that students may decline the federal service obligation and simply repay the tuition assistance and stipend as though they had been loans.

- **Targeted training.** As mentioned in the previous chapter, the CDC received statutory authority under 42 U.S.C. 247B-8 to develop programs to train health professionals. One example is the Public Health Prevention Service, initiated in 1997 and enhanced in July 2000, to provide master's-degree-level public health professionals with training and rotational work assignments at the CDC and at state and local health departments. The program is designed to train about 25 health professionals per year, who are then employed in the local, state, and federal public health workforce.

In addition, there is a civil-service wide (not STEM-specific) loan forgiveness program that is administered by OPM. OPM tracks the use of this program, which all federal agencies have authority (but not necessarily the funding) to use. In 2002, 690 federal employees availed themselves of the federal loan repayment program, about 20 percent of whom were STEM workers (Office of Personnel Management, 2002).

Retention
There are a variety of mechanisms for retaining STEM employees. Two principal ones are promotion and longevity pay raises. The retention bonus is another potentially useful mechanism for agencies facing sizable retirement eligibility in their workforce.

Employee Training and Skills Development
Training the current STEM workforce involves providing workers with additional needed STEM skills. One federal program focused on accomplishing this objective is the Dwight David Eisenhower Fellowship Program, which is administered somewhat differently by various agencies. For example, the Department of Transportation makes funds available to train state and local transportation employees (authorized by the Transportation Equity Act of 2001).

NIH's workforce planning documents indicate that workers affected by restructuring or budget cuts will be allowed to seek career counseling and retraining as necessary.[14]

Workplace Acculturation

Acculturation refers to influencing the values, attitudes, and awareness of organizational needs of members of the STEM workforce. The U.S. military has made some use of this mechanism to enhance the effectiveness of strategic planning (Levy et al., 2001).

Some federal institutions with special STEM missions (e.g., the Super Computer Research Center at Fort Meade is a notable example) have made particular accommodations for scientists and those in scientific career paths by enabling them to retain some focus on disciplinary interests that may not be directly connected to their specific job functions.

Illustrative Legislation

National Science Foundation Act (1950). Since its creation in 1950, the National Science Foundation has been the lead federal agency for promoting STEM education at all levels, with an emphasis on higher education. NSF also funds partnership programs that support multiple levels of the education system simultaneously. NSF is the only federal agency with specific legislative authority to create broadly targeted STEM workforce development initiatives (NIH has this authority in health fields, while other agencies have such authority in specific fields related to their missions). Several of NSF's current programs are aimed at workforce development. Only one of these explicitly pays for education in return for government employment, namely the NSF-funded Cyber Service Scholarships program. Some other NSF programs focusing on workforce development are the Advanced Technical Education program, Computer Science, Engineering, and Mathematics Scholarships, and the NSF Collaboratives for Excellence in Teacher Preparation.

---

[14]See http://www1.od.nih.gov/ohrm/PROGRAMS/WF-Plng/nih-plan/nih-wfp.pdf.

Women and Minorities in Science Act (1997). This law focused a great deal of attention on the underrepresentation of women and minorities in STEM fields. It did not, however, establish any specific programs or set aside funds to address the problem. Instead, it created a commission to study the issue and make recommendations. NSF issued a report on its findings in 2002. One result of the report was the creation of the Building Engineering and Science Talent (BEST) organization, a public-private partnership "dedicated to building a stronger, more diverse workforce."[15] The organization is studying best practices for encouraging women and minority scientists to pursue STEM careers. It is conducting a systematic assessment of best practices and is expected to complete its evaluation in 2004, when it will issue a comprehensive report. Eight federal agencies currently contribute funds to BEST, including NSF, Department of Commerce, DOE, NASA, DoD, Department of Education, and U.S. Department of Agriculture.

Paradigm Legislation? The National Defense Education Act of 1958

The Congress finds that an educational emergency exists and requires action by the federal government. Assistance will come from Washington to help develop as rapidly as possible those skills essential to the national defense.
—*The National Defense Education Act of 1958*

We now turn to a discussion of the effectiveness of the various mechanisms for influencing the size and composition of the STEM workforce. As an introduction to the subject, we will digress briefly to discuss the NDEA in some detail. The NDEA is especially relevant to the discussion because it employed essentially the full range of "pipeline-filling" mechanisms. The NDEA was the first major legislative initiative to address STEM education across all fields. In fact, its

---

[15] See http://www.bestworkforce.org for more information.

scope was broader than that—it was actually directed toward the entire U.S. education system, not just the education of those pursuing education for careers in STEM fields.

Background on the NDEA

The Soviet launch of Sputnik 1 and Sputnik 2 in the fall of 1957 shocked Americans and aroused deep anxiety about the state of the U.S. science and technology enterprise. Since the Second World War, Americans had been convinced that their national security was closely tied to the country's technological and scientific preeminence. The launch of the first Sputnik jolted Americans out of their complacency. Public attention quickly focused on the U.S. educational system, which bore the brunt of public blame for the nation falling behind the Russians in scientific achievement

The NDEA was passed in response to Sputnik. However, many of the concerns it addressed predated Sputnik. Education reform and the need for an expanded federal presence in education had been debated for years before the creation of the NDEA. One of the main concerns in the 1950s with the U.S. education system was inequality of funding that resulted from strictly local control of schools. The uneven tax base of different jurisdictions meant that school funding varied significantly across districts. Because of concerns about this inequality of funding and the levels of higher-education preparedness of America's burgeoning college-bound K–12 population, support for a greater federal role in financing and reshaping the U.S. education system had been building for years.

As Clowse (1981) notes, every provision of the NDEA had been introduced and debated by Congress before Sputnik was launched. What Sputnik provided, however, was a crisis that crystallized the political support that education reformers had been lacking and demolished their political opposition. Connecting education with national security provided the NDEA's Congressional proponents with a powerful argument for the need for the federal government to act. In September 1958, just 11 months after Sputnik, the NDEA passed both houses of Congress and was signed into law by President Eisenhower.

What did the NDEA actually do? The bill was a composite of programs to strengthen the U.S. education system by infusing federal resources at all levels, from primary to graduate school. The NDEA provided $4 billion over four years for education and related activities at all levels of the educational system, including the following:

- It gave school districts matching grants to buy classroom science equipment and equip libraries for K–12 public and private schools.
- It gave funds to state education agencies to train and test high school guidance counselors. The purpose of this provision was to steer talented youth toward college (although not toward STEM fields specifically).
- It gave funding to universities to:
    - Establish research and training centers for instruction in less-commonly taught languages and area studies.
    - Offer student loans of $1,000 maximum per year, up to $4,000 total, with "preference given to students with aptitude in science." Undergraduates who eventually pursued teaching careers were eligible to have 50 percent of their loan amounts forgiven, in increments of 10 percent per year of teaching.
    - Offer 5,500 three-year graduate fellowships to students enrolled in new or expanded programs, with the express purpose of steering graduates into college and university teaching. These fellowships were designed to alleviate an expected shortage of STEM teachers. The NDEA set out to increase the supply of science teachers by requiring universities to expand their Ph.D. programs in order to receive fellowship aid.
    - Conduct summer and full-year institutes for teachers in a variety of fields.
    - Propose innovative curricular ideas and materials.
    - Construct educational facilities.

The funds authorized by the NDEA were allotted to all states according to a college-population-based formula. The Act also contained explicit language barring any form of federal government control over local education.

Impact of the NDEA

There has been little systematic evaluation of the NDEA's success in strengthening the U.S. education system or its broader impact on the competitiveness of the country as a whole. Historians generally agree that it was a watershed law, whose principal significance was the precedent it set for federal involvement in K–12 education.[16] There has also been little assessment of the individual provisions of the NDEA. The scant assessment that exists suggests the following:

- The loan program was widely used by undergraduates. There is no convincing evidence, however, that loan forgiveness provisions induced borrowers to become teachers.
- Most school districts participated in the NDEA's equipment and materials program. The matching funds requirements presented a problem, however, especially for poor districts, where funds were often diverted from other programs. Schools also reportedly failed to keep pace with instructional technology after the initial investment because they did not in general purchase upgrades or improvements needed to keep abreast of technological improvements.
- The counseling programs, which provided counseling for students in grades 7 through 12, proved to be very popular and were expanded to include K–6 and college-level counseling. It is estimated that at least 3.5 million U.S. students at all levels were assisted by counseling programs developed from NDEA funds. The relevance of these programs to advances in STEM fields is unclear, however.

---

[16] This summary of evaluations of the NDEA is based on Forbis (1982).

- Graduate fellowships for college teaching were also fruitful. Program completion rates were high, and a large percentage of participants became college teachers.
- Funding for foreign language institutes was also successful and has continued through subsequent programs. As McDonnell et al. (1981, p. 1) note, the NDEA's international studies provisions have "profoundly shaped international education in this country."
- Teacher institutes, which existed before NDEA but were funded at much more modest levels, were perceived to be successful. They increased the knowledge of subject matter specialists and secondary teachers. Summer institutes remain popular today.

Overall, the NDEA has been judged to be an extraordinarily successful legislative initiative. One measure of its success is the swiftness with which its impact was felt. As Montgomery (1994) wrote, "The curricula developed under NSF programs were implemented with such speed and reach that by 1965, fully 50 percent of all high school physics students (200,000) were using the [NSF-developed] materials and 325,000 were employing NSF-sponsored chemistry curricula. Two years later, 3 million students were using these and other related material. In less than a single decade, American science education underwent a complete reformulation. Government money flowed in three critical directions: (1) to curriculum design groups; (2) to summer institutes for teacher training; and (3) to local school districts for the exclusive purchase of new curriculum material and equipment for science."

Is the NDEA Applicable Today?

The NDEA addressed the challenges of a different era. It inaugurated federal participation in an arena in which the federal government is still a major actor. Virtually all of the activities funded by the NDEA—student loan programs, scholarships, summer institutes, and foreign language training centers—are still funded by the federal government today, typically on a much larger scale than in the 1950s and 1960s.

Like most of today's federal STEM programs, the NDEA's provisions focused mainly on the pipeline for STEM workers rather than on the workforce itself. The Act did little to bridge school and workplace. The NDEA's supporters assumed that STEM graduates would find jobs, as the bill provided no workforce shaping incentives, except for its modest loan forgiveness provisions for teachers. To the extent that the federal government addressed STEM labor market issues at the time, it did so by means other than the NDEA. For instance, it substantially increased spending on government R&D programs, which in turn stimulated demand for STEM research careers, and created new federal agencies (NASA) and programs to fund them. In sum, measures to address the STEM workforce directly will find little precedent or guidance in the provisions of the NDEA.

One interesting facet of the NDEA that seemed to have disappeared in the late 1960s, but which is now reappearing in the form of university-school partnerships, is the active interest of university STEM professionals (who typically focus on their own research) in STEM education and curriculum design for K–12 schools. As Dow (1991) observes, the period after the passage of the NDEA may be the only time in American history in which university scientists took such a keen interest in K–12 curriculum development. NDEA was implemented in a way that made this happen. Although most of NDEA's K–12 provisions were administered during the 1950s and 1960s by the Office of Education in the Department of Health, Education, and Welfare, the curriculum development funds were administered through NSF, which awarded them as competitive grants via its usual peer-review process. The resulting awards went to university scientists, who proceeded to transform K–12 curricula and textbooks. Given current concerns with the teaching of K–12 science and math, university-school partnerships appear to be growing in importance and may be promising avenues for strengthening math and science teaching.

The NDEA was aimed primarily at improving K–12 science and math education, with the ultimate goal of producing scientifically trained specialists. This goal represents a fundamental difference between the concerns addressed by the NDEA and those addressed by today's federal K–12 STEM programs. The latter tend to focus on raising the overall level of scientific and technological literacy for the general student population. It seems likely that these two different goals are compatible, but they may call for different types of facilitating mechanisms.

Assessing the Effectiveness of Various Mechanisms

Given the paucity of initiatives aimed specifically at shaping the size and composition of the federal STEM workforce, combined with the scarcity of data on federal STEM workers, it is not surprising that virtually no systematic evaluation has been done on the success of any federal mechanisms in this area. Although a comprehensive assessment of the various mechanisms for shaping the federal STEM workforce is beyond the scope of this report, some first-order observations can be made.

Federal Mechanisms Have Emphasized Filling the Pipeline

- The federal government has focused its effort on filling the STEM pipeline rather than managing the STEM workforce.
- As indicated in Chapter Two, the federal government's pipeline-filling measures have been largely successful in the aggregate. The federal government has created a mature institutional framework with well-designed implementation mechanisms refined by decades of experience. At the aggregate level, it has had a fair amount of success in addressing STEM worker supply issues, including those affecting minorities and women. As noted in the 2002 STEM Indicators (National Science Board, 2002a), "Long-term trends show that the proportion of women enrolled in all graduate STEM fields is increasing. In 1999, women constituted 59 percent of the graduate enrollment in social and behavioral sciences, 43 percent of the graduate enrollment in natural sciences, and 20 percent of the graduate enrollment in engineering. In addition, women in underrepresented minority groups have a higher proportion of graduate enrollment than

women in other groups; one-third of black graduate students in engineering and more than one-half of the black graduate students in natural sciences are women."

- Federal agencies appear to have the statutory authority they need to conduct pipeline-filling programs to address particular needs.

Workforce-Shaping Mechanisms Are Just Beginning to Be Used

- The federal government seems to have made relatively little use of workforce-shaping mechanisms, although, as stated earlier, this has varied by agency. NASA seems to be the most active agency in this area, using workforce planning tools and collecting detailed information on the career paths of its STEM workforce, while also rapidly responding to strategic shortages or needs with targeted measures. But other agencies are also addressing these issues. The Department of Transportation, for example, has begun to address workforce development. In May 2002, the agency convened a national summit to address workforce development in the transportation sector, both in industry and across all levels of government.[17] The findings from that meeting are being integrated into current agency workforce planning and practices.

- Because most civil-service STEM staffing is done at the agency level, there is not a great deal of experience in using workforce management mechanisms across the entire federal STEM workforce. In fact, cross-agency STEM workforce management initiatives are likely to require significant coordination and have proven difficult to implement. The Cyber Service Scholarships program is a case in point. It was created to establish university programs for training experts in cyber security, a new field of expertise growing in demand at several federal agencies. The federal government (through NSF) funded new cyber security programs at a dozen U.S. universities. The universities offered full tuition assistance and stipends for two years to students en-

---

[17] For information on DOT efforts at shaping its STEM workforce, see http://www.nhi.fhwa.dot.gov/transworkforce.

tering the program, and guaranteed those students summer internships and positions in the federal government upon graduation in return for two years of government service. The program has generated considerable interest, and its concept has elicited favorable feedback in both university and government quarters. However, the program has faced implementation problems. It was coordinated initially out of the National Security Council Staff in the White House, and was apparently not well publicized across the hiring agencies, which received confusing regulations from OPM regarding the program's implementation and no funding for the program. Job fairs for graduates were sparsely attended by potential agency employers. OPM also experienced problems with coordinating job placements. OPM was responsible for ensuring that graduates received internships and that each graduate received at least one job offer. Some graduates were placed in internships at one agency but were hired at another, while others were not placed at all. The program is currently being redesigned so that agencies have more say in candidate admissions and thus have a greater investment in particular candidates for federal positions (McLellan, 2003).

- Retaining STEM workers does not seem to be a major problem for the federal government. For example, retention rates are higher for DoD STEM workers than for STEM workers in general, as noted in Chapter Three. However, this situation could change as the contractor workforce assumes a greater proportion of federal STEM duties, thereby inducing STEM workers currently in the federal workforce to seek employment in the private sector's STEM workforce. Therefore, retention mechanisms are probably needed sparingly, in particular fields such as information technology.

- Given that most of today's STEM students graduate from college with substantial amounts of loan debt, some form of loan forgiveness or repayment would likely serve as an effective recruiting mechanism for a substantial portion of STEM graduates. The current federal program for loan repayment is available to all federal employees, but is not STEM-specific. Creating a

STEM-specific program would likely require legislation to re-solve potentially competing agency jurisdictions.[18]

---

[18] The situation with loan repayment programs in 2003 differs from the situation at the time the NDEA was passed. The rapidly increasing cost of college education, and significantly greater dependence on loans to finance it, make it likely today that measures to forgive student loan debt would be more attractive now than were similar measures enacted in 1958.

CHAPTER FIVE

Conclusions

Is There a Shortage of STEM Workers?

One primary question this study sought to answer is, are there current or imminent shortages in the U.S. STEM workforce? This question can be answered, "No," with a degree of confidence for workers with a graduate education.

Standard economic indicators and other data do not support the claim of a broad national shortage. Certain fields or sub-fields may develop shortages (e.g., rapidly growing fields such as IT) and should be closely monitored. However, the downturn in the fortunes of the IT field after the burst of the Internet bubble makes such shortages seem less likely, and unemployment figures in other STEM fields indicate the potential to alleviate any shortfall by retraining workers in those fields. Also, STEM workers will not be immune to employment variations over business cycles, although they tend to be less affected than other college graduates.

In any case, for the general population, almost any conceivable shortfall in workers in any STEM field can be made up quickly by selectively relaxing H-1B visa quotas and other immigration restrictions. Dire predictions of damaging shortages in the STEM workforce, such as those in the 2003 report of the National Science Board's Committee on Education and Human Resources, do not seem likely to happen. There seems to be as much reason for concern about developing surpluses—driven by fellowships, post-doctoral positions, and other mechanisms in the absence of complementary efforts to assure adequate job spaces—as there is for concern about shortfalls. The last half century's experience would caution that surpluses in most STEM fields are the more likely outcome.

The notion of a shortage in the federal STEM workforce is also not supported by the data, but these data on the federal STEM workforce, although they are much more up-to-date than the national counterpart, are less than satisfactory. In particular, they address only the civil service workforce to the exclusion of the contract workforce, and they are of limited granularity. It is certainly the case that many federal agencies believe there will be a problem in the near future as the number of STEM employees who are eligible for retirement increases, but indicators suggest that the situation will not be as bad as many people assert. Actual patterns of STEM workforce retirement are substantially different from patterns of retirement eligibility. Actual retirements tend to occur later for STEM workers than for others.

Very few federal agencies maintain formal forecasts of STEM workforce requirements. Of those that do, few if any produce forecasts consisting of anything more than rough projections based on extrapolations. This situation is exacerbated by the growing ability (and propensity) of the federal government to contract out STEM work, thereby decreasing the in-house, civil service requirements. We have found little data and no forecasts for this substantial portion of the STEM workforce in service to the federal government. Because the size and characteristics of the portion of this private-sector workforce that works on government contract are much more elastic than the size and characteristics of federal STEM workforce, and because such outsourcing may be subject to political attention, forecasting the adequacy of the private sector component of the STEM workforce may be considerably more difficult.

Mirroring this dearth of forecasts, we have found no comprehensive evaluation of the effectiveness of past legislation and programs that were aimed at increasing the federal STEM workforce. With respect to the two major types of federal mechanisms—(1) those aimed at filling the pipeline in educational and training facilities and (2) those aimed at shaping the workforce—we conclude that the federal mechanisms have focused primarily on filling the pipeline. These pipeline-filling measures have created a mature set of institutions with implementing mechanisms that have been refined by decades of experience. At the aggregate level, women and minority participants in the STEM workforce have increased, which is presumably at least partly due to these mechanisms. Overall, federal agencies appear to have the statutory authority they need to conduct pipeline-filling programs to address particular needs.

With respect to workforce-shaping mechanisms, the federal government has been less ambitious and less successful, although again this situation has varied by agency. Because most civil service STEM staffing is done at the agency level, there is little precedent for or experience in using workforce-shaping mechanisms across the entire federal STEM workforce. In fact, cross-agency STEM workforce management initiatives are likely to require significant and challenging coordination. However, cross-agency management efforts are not needed to address all workforce-shaping issues. For example, retaining STEM workers does not seem to be a major problem for the federal government, implying that special retention mechanisms are needed only in certain agencies, and only in certain high-demand fields. However, there appear to be opportunities for workforce-shaping mechanisms in other areas, such as recruiting.

Given that many STEM students graduate with sizable loan debt, some form of loan forgiveness or repayment would likely serve as an effective recruiting mechanism for a substantial portion of STEM graduates. It is not clear, however, that such programs are widely needed.

The Need for Improved Data

Perceptions, rumors, and formal statements of STEM workforce shortfalls are in most cases not supported by the data. In fact, what data do exist seem to refute these assertions. However, the fact that these concerns exist implies that the situation should be monitored. To do so in a useful and timely manner will require improved data collection and reporting. To sketch a broad outline of such a data collection plan, we introduce two terms that capture important concepts: "spaces"—the requirements for workers with a specific set of skill; and "faces"—the qualified persons actually filling the spaces.[1] To adequately monitor the federal STEM workforce, STEM leaders need to know both current and forecasted states of both spaces and faces across the federal government.

Data on Spaces

The federal government should be able to forecast the number of spaces it will have for all STEM specialties. This requirement demands an understanding of evolving technology and changes in government roles. Clearly, forecasts will rarely be completely accurate, but without them there is no sound basis for planning. For example, prior to September 2001, the FBI could not have predicted a huge additional counter-terrorism requirement, but would still have needed to have plans to develop its workforce.

Data on future spaces will need to be consolidated in, or accessible from, a central location. All agencies might be required to develop and maintain forecasts for a reasonable number of years into the future. The federal government can develop alternative methods for doing this and share those methods with all departments and agencies. Additionally, attention should be paid to changes in the civil service–contractor mix in the federal STEM workforce, particularly if the current trend toward outsourcing federal workers continues.

Data on Faces

The data needed to adequately determine the ability of the national STEM workforce to supply the faces for filling the forecasted federal

---

[1] Our use of the "spaces" and "faces" terminology is not meant to assume that employers have fixed requirements for workers or that the definition of a qualified person is not subject to change. We presume that workforce requirements projections and data will take market and personnel flexibility into account to the maximum extent possible. So, for example, when faced with worker shortages, employers may redefine work and outsource some of it globally. Conversely, when there is an oversupply of highly skilled workers, employers may raise requirements for positions.

spaces are discussed in part in Chapter Three. Forecast models for this national workforce are maintained by the Bureau of Labor Statistics. Other means for filling STEM spaces (e.g., retraining workers into STEM specialties) should be considered in these models, as well as foreign workers and the output of standard education programs.

The broad patterns of STEM workforce requirements and availability reported here have emerged despite data that are not well suited to this purpose. More-targeted investigations for particular STEM specialties, particular agency employers, or particular geographic regions or demographic groups would likely founder.

Data on the U.S. STEM Workforce

The following are the major data deficiencies that hamper a more firmly grounded and finely grained analysis than the analysis we were able to conduct:

Lack of Timeliness
- Publication of consistent data on major characteristics of the national STEM workforce often occurs more than two years after the fact.

Lack of Comparability
- Characterization of workers by area of formal education ("face" in our nomenclature) or job classification ("space") is inconsistent in the data.

Inconsistent Definitions
- Data from different sources feature varying definitions, time domains, and levels of disaggregation. This inconsistency also makes comparability more difficult to establish.
- Important data series have experienced changing definitions without reported crosswalks or even documentation.

Lack of Data
- Data on years to Ph.D. degree are not consistently available by discipline.
- Earnings, unemployment, underemployment, and other economic indicators of a shortage or surplus are not available consistently for the STEM workforce and its components.

- Data are unavailable on numbers of STEM workers in other than STEM spaces.
- There are no "flash" indicators (available with, say, a one-quarter lag) of numbers of STEM students, proportion of foreign students, and numbers of STEM "spaces" in the federal government and private sector by major discipline and by selected critical sub-disciplines. Such indicators could provide an early warning of possible coming shortages or surpluses, thereby permitting STEM workforce managers to take appropriate steps (e.g., monitoring of a particular situation).

Data on the Federal Workforce

Relevant issues regarding data for the federal workforce are similar but not identical to those for the broader U.S. STEM workforce. As we have noted, OPM data on the federal workforce are much more timely than those available on the national workforce. They are also reasonably consistent across agencies. However, there are inconsistencies and gaps at the agency level and very little information on projections of future needs.

Inconsistent and Incomplete Data

- Consistent data are lacking on workforce retraining to meet STEM requirements.
- Current and historical demographic data on age, qualification level, and average age at retirement of STEM workers are incomplete.
- Few agencies maintain data on numbers and characteristics of the STEM workforce indirectly engaged through the A-76 mechanism or other outsourcing processes.
- Few agencies maintain forecasts of STEM worker requirements.

Lack of Data

- The data on STEM workers maintained by many agencies are no more detailed or complete than the data kept by the OPM.
- Data are unavailable on interagency mobility of STEM workers.

- There are no "flash" indicators (available with, say, a one-quarter lag)[2] of numbers of STEM students, proportion of foreign students, and numbers of STEM "spaces" in the federal government and private sector by major discipline and by selected critical sub-disciplines. Such indicators could provide an early warning of possible coming shortages or surpluses, thereby permitting STEM workforce managers to take appropriate steps (e.g., monitoring of a particular situation).
- There are no data available on the time interval between the government's decision to fill a STEM vacancy and its time of hiring a STEM worker to fill that vacancy. These data would shed light on the frequent claim that the federal government's long hiring time lags put it at a disadvantage relative to the private sector.

Some of these deficiencies are more constraining than others, depending on the particular focus of monitoring or analysis. Some are more easily corrected than others, depending on whether the cause of difficulty is at the source of the data or in the aggregation and reporting of the data. Establishing priorities, assigning responsibility, providing resources, coordinating data collection efforts, and monitoring progress have been successfully undertaken in other areas of federal statistics and may well be no more difficult for STEM workforce data.

The improvements that would result from these recommendations, when embodied in specific data with specified sources and methods, would permit statistical models to forecast STEM workforce trends in a comprehensive and timely manner and permit

---

[2] That is, there are no short turnaround indicators of pending shortages or surpluses that can quickly direct policymakers' attention to potential problem areas. These so-called flash indicators could provide early warning as quickly as three months after the fact. Additional in-depth data would then be gathered on these particular problem areas to decide whether the potential problems are serious or not. In the meantime, policy solutions would be at the ready. Such flash indicators might be developed for numbers of STEM students, proportions of foreign students, and numbers of STEM "spaces" in the federal government and private sector in selected critical subdisciplines.

the comparison of requirements (space forecasts) with personnel (face forecasts). Scientifically supportable policy decisions on STEM workforce mechanisms would be facilitated, as would informed training and career decisions by students and their advisors. Both personnel shortages with their attendant risks for the nation and personnel surpluses with their costs and disruptions for trained workers can thereby be reduced.

Bibliography

Adamson, David, and Gabrielle Bloom, interview with Department of Agriculture representatives, May 23, 2003.

Adamson, David, and Gabrielle Bloom, interview with Department of Transportation representatives, April 23, 2003.

American Association for the Advancement of Science (AAAS), *R&D Indicators, 2003*, Washington, D.C.: AAAS, 2003.

Bureau of Labor Statistics, "Employment Status of the Civilian Non-Institutional Population," 1940 to Date (available at http://www.bls.gov/cps/cpsaat1.pdf as of January 2004).

Butz, William P., G. A. Bloom, M. E. Gross, T. K. Kelly, A. Kofner, and H. E. Rippen, *Is There a Shortage of Scientists and Engineers? How Would We Know?* Santa Monica, Calif.: RAND Corporation, IP-241-OSTP, 2003 (available at http://www.rand.org/publications/IP/IP241/IP241.pdf as of January 2004).

Butz, William, and Donna Fossum, interview with OMB representative, April 18, 2003.

Butz, William, and Gabrielle Bloom, interview with OPM representatives, April 15, 2003.

Clowse, B. B., *Brainpower for the Cold War: The Sputnik Crisis and National Defense Education Act of 1958,* Westport, Conn.: Greenwood Press, 1981.

Day, J. C., and E. C. Newburger, *The Big Payoff: Educational Attainment and Synthetic Estimates of Work-Life Earnings,* Washington, D.C.: U.S. Census Bureau, Current Population Reports, 2002.

Department of Health and Human Services, Centers for Disease Control and Prevention and the Agency for Toxic Substances and Disease

Registry Representatives' written responses to RAND Interview Questions, May 21, 2003.

Department of Transportation, Federal Highway Administration, personal communication with DoT officials, April 23, 2003.

Douglass, J. A., "A Certain Future: Sputnik, American Higher Education, and the Survival of a Nation," in R. Launius, ed., *Reconsidering Sputnik: Forty Years Since the Soviet Satellite*, The Netherlands: Harwood Academic Publishers, 2000, pp. 327–362.

Dow, P. B., *Schoolhouse Politics: Lessons for the Sputnik Era*, Cambridge, Mass.: Harvard University Press, 1991.

Eitelberg, Deborah, and Vince Lauter, Defense Management Data Center (DMDC), *Briefing Charts: Retirement Trends: Scientists & Engineers vs All Other DoD Civilians*, Seaside, Calif.: DMDC, August 2002.

——, *Briefing Charts: STEM Attrition, Reasons Why Civilian Scientists and Engineers in RDT&E and Non-RDT&E Activities Left Civil Service Between June 2000–December 2001*, Seaside, Calif.: DMDC, August 2002b.

Federal Support for University Research: Forty Years After the National Defense Education Act and the Establishment of NASA, background for a one-day conference, University of California, Berkeley (available at http://ishi.lib.berkeley.edu/cshe/ndea/info.html as of January 2004).

FedScope Web site, Federal Human Resources Data, U.S. Office of Personnel Management (available at http://www.fedscope.opm.gov/index.htm as of January 2004).

Forbis, J. K., *Precollege Science and Mathematics Education: Experiences with the National Defense Education Act and the Teacher Institutes Conducted by the National Science Foundation*, Washington, D.C.: Congressional Research Service, 82-214 S, December 15, 1982.

Fossum, Donna, and Gabrielle Bloom, interview with NASA representatives, May 5, 2003.

Friel, B., "It's Time to Deflate the Overblown Rhetoric About Federal Staffing Problems," *Government Executive*, May 2003, pp. 21–32.

Friend, C., "What Promotes the Development of Women Scientists in Academia?" in C. C. Selby, ed., *Women in Science and Engineering: Choices for Success*, New York: Annals of the New York Academy of Sciences, Vol. 869, 1999, pp. 207–209.

General Services Administration, Office of Governmentwide Policy, Office of Acquisition Policy, Regulatory and Federal Assistance Publication

Division, *Catalog of Federal Domestic Assistance,* Washington, D.C.: GSA 2002 (available at http://12.46.245.173/cfda/cfda.html as of January 2004).

Goldman, Charles, and William Massy, *The Ph.D. Factory: Training and Employment of Science and Engineering Doctorates in the United States,* Bolton, Mass.: Anker Publishing, 1999.

Gross, Mihal, and Donna Fossum, interview with Department of Energy representatives, April 15, 2003.

Health Resources and Services Administration, U.S. Department of Health and Human Services, *Bureau of Health Professionals* Web site (available at http://bhpr.hrsa.gov/publichealth/phtc.htm as of January 2004).

Heylin, M., "Salaries Up But Jobs Still Tight," *Chemical and Engineering News,* Vol. 77, No. 31, August 2, 1999, pp. 28–39 (available at http://pubs.acs.org/cgi-bin/bottomframe.cgi?7731salary as of January 2004).

Heylin, M., "ChemCensus 2000," *Chemical and Engineering News,* Vol. 78, No. 33, August 14, 2000, pp. 46–53 (available at http://pubs.acs.org/cen/coverstory/7833/7833survey.html as of January 2004).

Horrigan, M., Bureau of Labor Statistics, U.S. Department of Labor, personal communication, 2003.

Institute of Medicine, *Reshaping the Graduate Education of Scientists and Engineers,* Washington, D.C.: National Academy Press, 1995.

Jackson, S., *The Quiet Crisis: Falling Short in Producing American Scientific and Technical Talent,* Washington, D.C.: BEST (Building Engineering and Science Talent), September 2002.

Jesse, J. K., "Education and Human Resources in the FY 2003 Budget," *AAAS Report XXVI: Research and Development, FY 2003,* Washington, D.C.: AAAS, 2002.

Kelly, Terrence, and David Adamson, interview with P. Albright, Assistant Secretary for Plans, Programs, and Budgets, Department of Homeland Security, May 19, 2003.

Kilburn, M. R., and B. J. Asch (eds.), *Recruiting Youth in the College Market: Current Practices and Future Policy Options,* Santa Monica, Calif.: RAND Corporation, MR-1093-OSD, 2003.

Levy, D. G., H. J. Thie, A. A. Robbert, S. Naftel, C. Cannon, R. H. Ehrenberg, and M. Gershwin, *Characterizing the Future Defense Workforce,* Santa Monica, Calif.: RAND Corporation, MR-1304-OSD, 2001.

Light, P. C., *The True Size of Government,* Washington, D.C.: Brookings Institution Press, 1999.

Loftsgaarden, D. O., J. W. Maxwell, and K. R. Priestley, "2001 Annual Survey of the Mathematical Sciences, Second Report," *Notices of the AMS,* Vol. 49, No. 7, August 2002, pp. 803–816 (available at: http://www.ams.org/notices/200207/01second-report.pdf as of January 2004).

McDonnell, L. S., E. Berryman, M. D. Scott, J. A. Pincus, and A. Eisenshtat Robyn, *Federal Support for International Studies: The Role of NDEA Title VI,* Santa Monica, Calif.: RAND Corporation, R-2770-ED, 1981.

McLellan, V., "Cyber Corps' Failing Grades," *Information Security* Web site, June 2003 (available at http://infosecuritymag.techtarget.com/2003/jun/cybercorps.shtml as of January 2004).

Montgomery, S. L., *Minds for the Making: The Role of Science in American Education, 1750–1990,* New York: Guilford Press, 1994.

NASA Workforce Web site, Office of Human Resources, National Aeronautics and Space Administration (available at http://nasapeople.nasa.gov/workforce/data/page4.htm as of January 2004).

National Academy of Public Administration, *The Transforming Power of Information Technology: Making the Federal Government an Employer of Choice for IT Employees,* Washington, D.C.: National Academy of Public Administration, 2001.

National Institutes of Health, U.S. Department of Health and Human Services, *Workforce Plan,* FY2002 and FY2003, June 2001 (available at http://www1.od.nih.gov/ohrm/PROGRAMS/WF-Plng/nih-plan/nih-wfp.pdf as of January 2004).

National Research Council, *Forecasting the Demand and Supply of Scientists and Engineers,* Washington, D.C.: National Academy Press, 2000a.

National Research Council, Office of Scientific and Engineering Personnel, *Measuring the Science and Engineering Enterprise: Priorities for the Division of Science Resources Studies,* Washington, D.C.: National Academy Press, 2000b.

National Research Council, *Building a Workforce for the Information Economy,* Washington, D.C.: National Academy Press, 2001.

National Research Council, *Trends in the Early Careers of Life Scientists,* Washington, D.C.: National Academy Press, 1998.

National Science Board, *Science and Engineering Indicators—1993,* Arlington, VA: National Science Foundation (NSB 93-1), 1993.

——, *Science and Engineering Indicators—2002, Volume I*, Arlington, Va.: National Science Foundation (NSB 02-1), 2002a (available at http://www.nsf.gov/sbe/srs/seind02/start.htm).

——, *Science and Engineering Indicators—2002, Volume II, Appendix Tables*, Arlington, VA: National Science Foundation (NSB 02-1), 2002b (available at http://www.nsf.gov/sbe/srs/seind02/start.htm).

——, *The Science and Engineering Workforce: Realizing Americ"'s Potential*, Arlington, VA: Committee on Education and Human Resources, Task Force on National Workforce Policies for Science and Engineering (NSB 03-69), 2003.

National Science Foundation, *Science and Engineering Degrees 1966–1994*, Arlington, Va.: NSF, NSF-96-321, 1996.

National Science Foundation, Division of Science Resources Statistics, *SESTA—Scientists and Engineers Statistical Data System* Web site (available at http://srsstats.sbe.nsf.gov/ as of January 2004).

National Science and Technology Council, *Ensuring a Strong U.S. Scientific, Technical, and Engineering Workforce in the 21st Century*, Washington, D.C.: Office of Science and Technology Policy, 2000 (available at http://www.ostp.gov/html/00411_3.html as of December 2003).

O'Connell, C. F., Jr., "The Corps of Engineers and the Rise of Modern Management, 1827–1856," in M. R. Smith, ed., *Military Enterprise and Technological Change: Perspectives on the American Experience*, Cambridge, Mass.: MIT Press, 1985.

Office of Management and Budget, *Performance of Commercial Activities*, Circular A-76, Washington, D.C.: OMB, revised May 29, 2003 (available at http://www.whitehouse.gov/omb/circulars/a076/a76_rev2003.pdf as of January 2004).

Office of Personnel Management, *Federal Student Loan Repayment Program, Fiscal Year 2002, Report to Congress*, Washington, D.C.: OPM (available at http://www.opm.gov/oca/PAY/StudentLoan/HTML/Report.ASP as of January 2004).

Office of Technology Assessment, *Educating Scientists and Engineers: Grade School to Grad School*, Washington, D.C.: U.S. Congress, OTA-SET-377, June 1988 (available on Princeton University's Web archive at http://www.wws.princeton.edu/cgi-bin/byteserv.prl/~ota/ns20/year_f.html as of January 2004).

Rudolph, F., *The American College and University: A History,* Athens, Ga.: University of Georgia Press, 1962.

Sargent, J., "The U.S. Science and Engineering Workforce," PowerPoint presentation, United States Department of Commerce, Washington, D.C., April 1, 2003.

Scientist and Engineers Statistical Data System (SESTAT), "SESTAT Detailed Statistical Tables," 1993–1999 (available at http://srsstats.sbe. nsf.gov/).

U. S. Department of Labor, Bureau of Labor Statistics, *Industry Report: Occupation Projections,* available at http://data.bls.gov/servlet/oep.nioem. servlet.ActionServlet?Action=empior&MultipleSelect=XXXXXX&Sort= ws_emp_b&StartItem=0&Resort=No&ResortButton=No&Base=2000 &Proj=2010&SingleSelect=909100&Type=Industry&Number=All.

U.S. House of Representatives, Committee on Science, Space, and Technology, Subcommittee on Investigations and Oversight, *Projecting Science and Engineering Personnel Requirements for the 1990s: How Good are the Numbers?* Washington, D.C.: U.S. Government Printing Office, 1993, pp. 1–10.

"U.S. Immigration Reform: Positive or Negative? Business, Labor Will Work to Different Agendas in Upcoming Debate," *Semiconductor Magazine,* Vol. 3, No. 1, January 2002.

Williams, V. L., *Merging University Students into K–12 Science Education Reform,* Santa Monica, Calif.: RAND Corporation, MR-1446-NSF, 2002.